HARD QUESTIONS ABOUT
Creation

Only A. Guy

Published by VIP Ink Publishing, L.L.C.
www.vipinkpublishing.com

Cover Design and Book Layout by Sarah McClain.
www.thewritesarah.com

Guy, Only A.
Hard Questions About Creation
First Edition Print

ISBN 13: 978-1-939670-06-9
ISBN: 978-1-939670-06-9
Printed in the USA.

1. Question:
"What does the Bible say about Creation vs. evolution?"

Answer: It is not the purpose of this answer to present a scientific argument in the creation vs. evolution debate. For scientific arguments for creation and/or against evolution, we highly recommend Answers in Genesis and the Institute for Creation Research. The purpose of this article is to explain why, according to the Bible, the creation vs. evolution debate even exists. Romans 1:25 declares, *"They exchanged the truth of God for a lie, and worshiped and served created things rather than the Creator—who is forever praised. Amen."*

A key factor in the debate is that the majority of scientists who believe in evolution are also atheists or agnostics. There are some who hold to some form of theistic evolution and others who take a deistic view of God (God exists but is not involved in the world, and everything proceeds along a natural course). There are some who genuinely and honestly look at the data and arrive at the conclusion that evolution better fits with the data. However, these represent an insignificant percentage of the scientists who advocate evolution. The vast majority of evolutionary scientists hold that life evolved entirely without any intervention of a higher being. Evolution is by definition a naturalistic science.

For atheism to be true, there must be an alternate explanation—other than a Creator—for how the universe and life came into existence. Although belief in some form of evolution predated Charles Darwin, he was the first to develop a plausible model for the process of evolution—natural selection. Darwin once identified himself as a Christian but as a result of some tragedies that took place in his life, he later renounced the Christian faith and the existence of God. Evolution was invented by an atheist. Darwin's goal was not to disprove God's existence, but that is one of the end results of the theory of evolution. Evolution is an enabler of atheism. Evolutionary scientists likely would not admit that their goal is to give an alternate explanation of the origins of life, and thereby to give a foundation for atheism, but according to the Bible, that is exactly why the theory of evolution exists.

The Bible tells us, *"The fool says in his heart, 'There is no God'"* (Psalm 14:1; 53:1). The Bible also proclaims that people are without excuse for not believing in a Creator God. *"For since the creation of the world God's invisible qualities—His eternal power and divine nature—have been clearly seen, being understood from what has been made, so that men are without excuse"* (Romans 1:20). According to the Bible, anyone who denies the existence of God is a fool. Why, then, are so many people, including some Christians, willing to accept that evolutionary scientists are unbiased interpreters of scientific data? According to the Bible, they are all fools! Foolishness does not imply a lack of intelligence. Most evolutionary scientists are brilliant intellectually. Foolishness indicates an inability to properly apply knowledge. Proverbs 1:7 tells us, *"The fear of the LORD is the beginning of knowledge, but fools despise wisdom and discipline."*

Evolutionary scientists mock creation and/or intelligent

design as unscientific and not worthy of scientific examination. In order for something to be considered a *"science,"* they argue, it must be able to be observed and tested; it must be *"naturalistic."* Creation is by definition *"supernatural."* God and the supernatural cannot be observed or tested (so the argument goes); therefore, creation and/or intelligent design cannot be considered science. Of course, neither can evolution be observed or tested, but that does not seem to be an issue with evolutionists. As a result, all data is filtered through the preconceived, presupposed, and pre-accepted theory of evolution, without alternate explanations being considered.

However, the origin of the universe and the origin of life cannot be tested or observed. Both creation and evolution are faith-based systems in regards to origins. Neither can be tested because we cannot go back billions (or thousands) of years to observe the origin of the universe or of life in the universe. Evolutionary scientists reject creation on grounds that would logically force them to also reject evolution as a scientific explanation of origins. Evolution, at least in regard to origins, does not fit the definition of *"science"* any more than creation does. Evolution is supposedly the only explanation of origins that can be tested; therefore, it is the only theory of origins that can be considered *"scientific."* This is foolishness! Scientists who advocate evolution are rejecting a plausible theory of origins without even honestly examining its merits, because it does not fit their illogically narrow definition of *"science."*

If creation is true, then there is a Creator to whom we are accountable. Evolution is an enabler for atheism. Evolution gives atheists a basis for explaining how life exists apart from a Creator God. Evolution denies the need for a God to be involved in the universe. Evolution is the *"creation theory"* for the religion of atheism. According to the Bible, the choice is clear. We can believe the Word of our omnipotent and omniscient God, or we can believe the illogically biased, *"scientific"* explanations of fools.

2. QUESTION:
"What does the Bible say about dinosaurs? Are there dinosaurs in the Bible?"

ANSWER: The topic of dinosaurs in the Bible is part of a larger ongoing debate within the Christian community over the age of the earth, the proper interpretation of Genesis, and how to interpret the physical evidences we find all around us. Those who believe in an older age for the earth tend to agree that the Bible does not mention dinosaurs, because, according to their paradigm, dinosaurs died out millions of years before the first man ever walked the earth. The men who wrote the Bible could not have seen living dinosaurs.

Those who believe in a younger age for the earth tend to agree that the Bible does mention dinosaurs, though it never actually uses the word *"dinosaur."* Instead, it uses the Hebrew word tanniyn, which is translated a few different ways in our English Bibles. Sometimes it's *"sea monster,"* and sometimes it's *"serpent."* It is most commonly translated *"dragon."* The tanniyn appear to have been some sort of giant reptile. These creatures are mentioned nearly thirty times in the Old Testament and were found both on land and in the water.

In addition to mentioning these giant reptiles, the Bible describes a couple of creatures in such a way that some scholars believe the writers may have been describing dinosaurs. The behemoth is said to be the mightiest of all God's creatures, a giant whose tail is likened to a cedar tree (Job 40:15). Some scholars have tried to identify the behemoth as either an elephant or a hippopotamus. Others point out that elephants and hippopotamuses have very thin tails, nothing comparable to a cedar tree. Dinosaurs like the brachiosaurus and the diplodocus, on the other hand, had huge tails which could easily be compared to a cedar tree.

Nearly every ancient civilization has some sort of art depicting giant reptilian creatures. Petroglyphs, artifacts, and even little clay figurines found in North America resemble modern depictions of dinosaurs. Rock carvings in South America depict men riding diplodocus-like creatures and, amazingly, bear the familiar images of triceratops-like, pterodactyl-like, and tyrannosaurus rex-like creatures. Roman mosaics, Mayan pottery, and Babylonian city walls all testify to man's trans-cultural, geographically unbounded fascination with these creatures. Sober accounts like those of Marco Polo's Il Milione mingle with fantastic tales of treasure-hoarding beasts. In addition to the substantial amount of anthropic and historical evidences for the coexistence of dinosaurs and man, there are physical evidences, like the fossilized footprints of humans and dinosaurs found together at places in North America and West-Central Asia.

So, are there dinosaurs in the Bible? The matter is far from settled. It depends on how you interpret the available evidences and how you view the world around you. If the Bible is interpreted literally, a young earth interpretation will result, and the idea that dinosaurs and man coexisted can be accepted. If dinosaurs and human beings coexisted, what happened to the dinosaurs? While the Bible does not discuss the issue, dinosaurs likely died out sometime after the flood due to a combination of dramatic environmental shifts and the fact that they were relentlessly hunted to extinction by man.

3. QUESTION:
"Does faith in God and science contradict?"

ANSWER: Science is defined as *"the observation, identification, description, experimental investigation, and theoretical explanation of phenomena."* Science is a method that mankind can use to gain a greater understanding of the natural universe. It is a search for knowledge through observation. Advances in science demonstrate the reach of human logic and imagination. However, a Christian's belief in science should never be like our belief in God. A Christian can have faith in God and respect for science, as long as we remember which is perfect and which is not.

Our belief in God is a belief of faith. We have faith in His Son for salvation, faith in His Word for instruction, and faith in His Holy Spirit for guidance. Our faith in God should be absolute, since when we put our faith in God, we depend on a perfect, omnipotent, omniscient Creator. Our belief in science should be intellectual and nothing more. We can count on science to do many great things, but we can also count on science to make mistakes. If we put faith in science, we depend on imperfect, sinful, limited, mortal men. Science throughout history has been wrong about many things, such as the shape of the earth, powered flight, vaccines, blood transfusions, and even reproduction. God is never wrong.

Truth is nothing to fear, so thee is no reason for a Christian to fear good science. Learning more about the way God constructed our universe helps all of mankind appreciate the wonder of creation. Expanding our knowledge helps us to combat disease, ignorance, and misunderstanding. However, there is danger when scientists hold their faith in human logic above faith in our Creator. These persons are no different from anyone devoted to a religion; they have chosen faith in man and will find facts to defend that faith.

Still, the most rational scientists, even those who refuse to believe in God, admit to a lack of completeness in our understanding of the universe. They will admit that neither God nor the Bible can be proved or disproved by science, just as many of their favorite theories ultimately cannot be proved or disproved. Science is meant to be a truly neutral discipline, seeking only the truth, not furtherance of an agenda.

Much of science supports the existence and work of God. Psalm 19:1 says, *"The heavens declare the glory of God; the skies proclaim the work of His hands."* As modern science discovers more about the universe, we find more evidence of creation. The amazing complexity and replication of DNA, the intricate and interlocking laws of physics, and the absolute harmony of conditions and chemistry here on earth all serve to support the message of the Bible. A Christian should embrace science that seeks the truth, but reject the *"priests of science"* who put human knowledge above God.

4. QUESTION:
"What is the age of the earth? How old is the earth?"

ANSWER: Given the fact that, according to the Bible, Adam was created on the sixth day of our planet's existence, we can determine a biblically-based, approximate age for the earth by looking at the chronological details of the human race. This assumes that the Genesis account is accurate, that the six days of creation were literal 24-hour periods, and that there were no ambiguous gaps in the chronology of Genesis.

The genealogies listed in Genesis chapters 5 and 11 provide the age at which Adam and his descendants each fathered the next generation in a successive ancestral line from Adam to Abraham. By determining where Abraham fits into history chronologically and adding up the ages provided in Genesis 5 and 11, it becomes apparent that the Bible teaches the earth to be about 6000 years old, give or take a few hundred years.

What about the billions of years accepted by most scientists today and taught in the vast majority of our academic institutions? This age is primarily derived from two dating techniques: radiometric dating and the geologic timescale. Scientists who advocate the younger age of about 6000 years insist that radiometric dating is flawed in that it is founded upon a series of faulty assumptions, while the geologic timescale is flawed in that it employs circular reasoning. Moreover, they point to the debunking of old-earth myths, like the popular misconception that it takes long periods of time for stratification, fossilization and the formation of diamonds, coal, oil, stalactites, stalagmites, etc, to occur. Finally, young-earth advocates present positive evidence for a young age for the earth in place of the old-earth evidences which they debunk. Young-earth scientists acknowledge that they are in the minority today but insist that their ranks will swell over time as more and more scientists reexamine the evidence and take a closer look at the currently accepted old-earth paradigm.

Ultimately, the age of the earth cannot be proven. Whether 6000 years or billions of years, both viewpoints (and everything in between) rest on faith and assumptions. Those who hold to billions of years trust that methods such as radiometric dating are reliable and that nothing has occurred in history that may have disrupted the normal decay of radio-isotopes. Those who hold to 6000 years trust that the Bible is true and that other factors explain the *"apparent"* age of the earth, such as the global flood, or God's creating the universe in a state that *"appears"* to give it a very long age. As an example, God created Adam and Eve as fully-grown adult human beings. If a doctor had examined Adam and Eve on the day of their creation, the doctor would have estimated their age at 20 years (or whatever age they appeared to be) when, in fact, Adam and Eve were less than one day old. Whatever the case, there is always good reason to trust the Word of God over the words of atheistic scientists with an evolutionary agenda.

5. QUESTION:
"Why are there two different Creation accounts in Genesis chapters 1-2?"

ANSWER: Genesis 1:1 says, *"In the beginning, God created the heavens and the earth."* Later, in Genesis 2:4, it seems that a second, different story of creation begins. The idea of two differing creation accounts is a common misinterpretation of these two passages which, in fact, describe the same creation event. They do not disagree as to the order in which things were created and do not contradict one another. Genesis 1 describes the *"six days of creation"* (and a seventh day of rest), Genesis 2 covers only one day of that creation week—the sixth day—and there is no contradiction.

In Genesis 2, the author steps back in the temporal sequence to the sixth day, when God made man. In the first chapter, the author of Genesis presents the creation of man on the sixth day as the culmination or high point of creation. Then, in the second chapter, the author gives greater detail regarding the creation of man.

There are two primary claims of contradictions between

Genesis chapters 1-2. The first is in regard to plant life. Genesis 1:11 records God creating vegetation on the third day. Genesis 2:5 states that prior to the creation of man *"no shrub of the field had yet appeared on the earth and no plant of the field had yet sprung up, for the LORD God had not sent rain on the earth and there was no man to work the ground."* So, which is it? Did God create vegetation on the third day before He created man (Genesis 1), or after He created man (Genesis 2)? The Hebrew words for *"vegetation"* are different in the two passages. Genesis 1:11 uses a term that refers to vegetation in general. Genesis 2:5 uses a more specific term that refers to vegetation that requires agriculture, i.e., a person to tend it, a gardener. The passages do not contradict. Genesis 1:11 speaks of God creating vegetation, and Genesis 2:5 speaks of God not causing *"farmable"* vegetation to grow until after He created man.

The second claimed contradiction is in regard to animal life. Genesis 1:24-25 records God creating animal life on the sixth day, before He created man. Genesis 2:19, in some translations, seems to record God creating the animals after He had created man. However, a good and plausible translation of Genesis 2:19-20 reads, *"Now the LORD God had formed out of the ground all the beasts of the field and all the birds of the air. He brought them to the man to see what he would name them, and whatever the man called each living creature, that was its name. So the man gave names to all the livestock, the birds of the air and all the beasts of the field."* The text does not say that God created man, then created the animals, and then brought the animals to the man. Rather, the text says, *"Now the LORD God had [already] created all the animals."* There is no contradiction. On the sixth day, God created the animals, then created man, and then brought the animals to the man, allowing the man to name the animals.

By considering the two creation accounts individually and then reconciling them, we see that God describes the sequence of creation in Genesis 1, then clarifies its most important details, especially of the sixth day, in Genesis 2. There is no contradiction here, merely a common literary device describing an event from the general to the specific.

6. QUESTION:
"Who was Cain's wife? Was Cain's wife his sister?"

ANSWER: The Bible does not specifically say who Cain's wife was. The only possible answer is that Cain's wife was his sister or niece or great-niece, etc. The Bible does not say how old Cain was when he killed Abel (Genesis 4:8). Since they were both farmers, they were likely both full-grown adults, possibly with families of their own. Adam and Eve surely had given birth to more children than just Cain and Abel at the time Abel was killed. They definitely had many more children later (Genesis 5:4). The fact that Cain was scared for his own life after he killed Abel (Genesis 4:14) indicates that there were likely many other children and perhaps even grandchildren of Adam and Eve already living at that time. Cain's wife (Genesis 4:17) was a daughter or granddaughter of Adam and Eve.

Since Adam and Eve were the first (and only) human beings, their children would have no other choice than to intermarry. God did not forbid inter-family marriage until much later when there were enough people to make intermarriage unnecessary (Leviticus 18:6-18). The reason that incest today often results in genetic abnormalities is that when two people of similar genetics (i.e., a brother and sister) have children together, there is a high risk of their recessive characteristics becoming dominant. When people from different families have children, it is highly unlikely that both parents will carry the same recessive traits. The human genetic code has become increasingly *"polluted"* over the centuries as genetic defects are multiplied, amplified, and passed down from generation to generation. Adam and Eve did not have any genetic defects, and that enabled them and the first few generations of their descendants to have a far greater quality of health than we do now. Adam and Eve's children had few, if any, genetic defects. As a result, it was safe for them to intermarry.

7. QUESTION:
"Who was Cain afraid of after he killed Abel?"

ANSWER: In Genesis 4:13-14, shortly after he killed his brother Abel, *"Cain said to the LORD, 'My punishment is more than I can bear. Today you are driving me from the land, and I will be hidden from your presence; I will be a restless wanderer on the earth, and whoever finds me will kill me.'"* Who exactly was Cain afraid of? The only people the book of Genesis had mentioned to this point are Adam and Eve (Cain's parents) and Abel (who was now dead). Who would possibly be a threat to Cain?

It is important to recognize that Cain and Abel were both full-grown adults at the time that Cain killed Abel. Both Cain and Abel were farmers, who tended to their own lands and flocks (Genesis 4:2-4). The Bible does not tell us how old Cain and Abel were, but they very likely could have been in their 30's or 40's. The Bible does not specifically mention Adam and Eve having any children between Abel and Seth (Genesis 4:25). However, it is highly unlikely that the two most perfect human beings in the history of the world, Adam and Eve, would not have any children over several decades. Adam and Eve had many children after Seth (Genesis 5:4), so why would they not also have had other children between Abel and Seth? The Bible does not say that Seth was Adam and Eve's first child, or even first son, after Abel was killed. Rather, it states that Seth was born as a *"replacement"* for Abel. Genesis chapter 5 traces the genealogy of Seth. Prior to his death, Abel was likely the *"chosen"* son that would eventually produce the Messiah (Genesis 3:15). It is in this sense that Seth "replaced" Abel.

So, who was Cain afraid of? Cain was afraid of his own brothers, sisters, nephews, and nieces, who were already born and would be capable of seeking revenge. The fact that Cain had a wife (Genesis 4:17) is a further evidence that Adam and Eve had other children after Cain and Abel, but before Seth.

8. QUESTION:
"What does the Bible say about cavemen, prehistoric men, Neanderthals?"

ANSWER: The Bible does not use the term *"caveman"* or *"Neanderthals,"* and according to the Bible there is no such thing as *"prehistoric"* man. The term *"prehistoric"* means *"belonging to the era before recorded history."* It presupposes that the biblical account is merely a fabrication, because the book of Genesis records events which precede the creation of man (namely, the first five days of creation—man was created on the sixth day). The Bible is clear that Adam and Eve were perfect humans from the time of their creation and did not evolve from lower life forms.

With that said, the Bible does describe a period of traumatic upheaval upon the earth—the flood (Genesis 6-9), during which time civilization was utterly destroyed except for eight people. Humanity was forced to start over. It is in this historical context that some scholars believe men lived in caves and made use of stone tools. These men were not primitive; they were simply destitute. And they certainly were not half ape. The fossil evidence is quite clear: cavemen were human—men who lived in caves.

There are some fossilized ape remains which Darwinian paleo-anthropologists interpret as being some sort of transition between ape and men. Most people seem to think of these interpretations when they imagine cavemen. They picture furry half-men, half-ape creatures crouched in a cave next to a fire, drawing on the walls with their newly developed stone tools. This is a common misconception. And as far as Darwinian paleo-anthropology goes, we should keep in mind that these interpretations reflect a peculiar worldview and are not the result of the evidence. In fact, not only is there major opposition to these interpretations within the academic community, the Darwinists themselves do not entirely agree with each other on the details.

Unfortunately, the popular mainstream view promotes this idea that man and ape both evolved from the same ancestor, but this is certainly not the only plausible interpretation of the available evidence. In fact, the evidence in favor of this particular interpretation is lacking.

When God created Adam and Eve, they were fully developed human beings, capable of communication, society, and development (Genesis 2:19-25; 3:1-20; 4:1-12). It is almost entertaining to consider the lengths evolutionary scientists go to prove the existence of prehistoric cavemen. They find a misshapen tooth in a cave and from that create a misshapen human being who lived in a cave, hunched over like an ape. There is no way that science can prove the existence of cavemen by a fossil. Evolutionary scientists simply have a theory, and then they force the evidence to fit the theory. Adam and Eve were the first human beings ever created and were fully-formed, intelligent, and upright.

9. QUESTION:
"Does Genesis chapter 1 mean literal 24-hour days?"

ANSWER: A careful examination of the Hebrew word for *"day"* and the context in which it appears in Genesis will lead to the conclusion that *"day"* means a literal, 24-hour period of time. The Hebrew word yom translated into the English "day" can mean more than one thing. It can refer to the 24-hour period of time that it takes for the earth to rotate on its axis (e.g., *"there are 24 hours in a day"*). It can refer to the period of daylight between dawn and dusk (e.g., *"it gets pretty hot during the day but it cools down a bit at night"*). And it can refer to an unspecified period of time (e.g., *"back in my grandfather's day..."*). It is used to refer to a 24-hour period in Genesis 7:11. It is used to refer to the period of daylight between dawn and dusk in Genesis 1:16. And it is used to refer to an unspecified period of time in Genesis 2:4. So, what does it mean in Genesis 1:5-2:2 when it's used in conjunction with ordinal numbers (i.e., the first day, the second day, the third day, the fourth day, the fifth day, the sixth day, and the seventh day)? Are these 24-hour periods or something else? Could yom as it is used here mean an unspecified period of time?

We can determine how yom should be interpreted in Genesis 1:5-2:2 simply by examining the context in which we find the word and then comparing its context with how we see its usage elsewhere in Scripture. By doing this we let Scripture interpret itself. The Hebrew word yom is used 2301 times in the Old Testament. Outside of Genesis 1, yom plus a number (used 410 times) always indicates an ordinary day, i.e., a 24-hour period. The words *"evening"* and *"morning"* together (38 times) always indicate an ordinary day. Yom + *"evening"* or *"morning"* (23 times) always indicates an ordinary day. Yom + *"night"* (52 times) always indicates an ordinary day.

The context in which the word yom is used in Genesis 1:5-2:2, describing each day as *"the evening and the morning,"* makes it quite clear that the author of Genesis meant 24-hour periods. The references to *"evening"* and *"morning"* make no sense unless they refer to a literal 24-hour day. This was the standard interpretation of the days of Genesis 1:5-2:2 until the 1800s when a paradigm shift occurred within the scientific community, and the earth's sedimentary strata layers were reinterpreted. Whereas previously the rock layers were interpreted as evidence of Noah's flood, the flood was thrown out by the scientific community and the rock layers were reinterpreted as evidence for an excessively old earth. Some well-meaning but terribly mistaken Christians then sought to reconcile this new anti-flood, anti-biblical interpretation with the Genesis account by reinterpreting yom to mean vast, unspecified periods of time.

The truth is that many of the old-earth interpretations are known to rely upon faulty assumptions. But we must not let the stubborn close-mindedness of some scientists influence how we read the Bible. According to Exodus 20:9-11, God used six literal days to create the world in order to serve as a model for man's workweek: work six days, rest one. Certainly God could have created everything in an instant if He wanted to. But apparently He had us in mind even before He made us (on the sixth day) and wanted to provide an example for us to follow.

10. QUESTION:
"What is theistic evolution?"

ANSWER: Theistic evolution is one of three major origin-of-life worldviews, the other two being atheistic evolution (also commonly known as Darwinian evolution and naturalistic evolution) and special creation.

Atheistic evolution says that there is no God and that life can and did emerge naturally from preexisting, non-living building blocks under the influence of natural laws (like gravity, etc), although the origin of those natural laws is not explained. Special creation says that God created life directly, either from nothing or from preexisting materials.

Theistic evolution says one of two things. The first option is that there is a God, but He was not directly involved in the origin of life. He may have created the building blocks, He may have created the natural laws, He may even have created these things with the eventual emergence of life in mind, but at some point early on He stepped back and let His creation take over. He let it do what it does, whatever that is, and life eventually emerged from non-living material. This view is similar to atheistic evolution in that it presumes a naturalistic origin of life.

The second alternative of theistic evolution is that God did not perform just one or two miracles to bring about the origin of life as we know it. His miracles were constant. He led life step by step down a path that took it from primeval simplicity to contemporary complexity, similar to Darwin's evolutionary tree of life (fish begot amphibians who begot reptiles who begot birds and mammals, etc). Where life was not able to evolve naturally (how does a reptile's limb evolve into a bird's wing naturally?), God stepped in. This view is similar to special creation in that it presumes that God acted supernaturally in some way to bring about life as we know it.

There are numerous differences between the biblical special creation perspective and the theistic evolution perspective. One significant difference concerns their respective views on death. Theistic evolutionists tend to believe that the earth is billions of years old and that the geologic column containing the fossil record represents long epochs of time. Since man does not appear until late in the fossil record, theistic evolutionists believe that many creatures lived, died, and became extinct long before man's belated arrival. This means that death existed before Adam and his sin.

Biblical creationists believe that the earth is relatively young and that the fossil record was laid down during and after Noah's flood. The stratification of the layers is thought to have occurred due to hydrologic sorting and liquefaction, both of which are observed phenomena. This puts the fossil record and the death and carnage which it describes hundreds of years after Adam's sin.

Another significant difference between the two positions is how they read Genesis. Theistic evolutionists tend to subscribe to either the day-age theory or the framework theory, both of which are allegorical interpretations of the Genesis 1 creation week. Young earth creationists subscribe to a literal 24-hour day as they read Genesis 1. Both of the theistic evolutionist views are flawed from a Christian perspective in that they do not line up with the Genesis creation account.

Theistic evolutionists imagine a Darwinian scenario in which stars evolved, then our solar system, then earth, then plants and animals, and eventually man. The two theistic evolution viewpoints disagree as to the role God played in the unfolding of events, but they generally agree on the Darwinian timeline. This timeline is in conflict with the Genesis creation account. For example, Genesis 1 says that the earth was created on day one and the sun, moon, and stars were not created until day four. Some argue that the wording of Genesis suggests the sun, moon, and stars were actually created on day one but they could not be seen through earth's atmosphere until day four, leading to their placement on day four. This is a bit of a stretch, as the Genesis account is pretty clear that the earth did not have an atmosphere until the second day. If the sun, moon, and stars were created on day one, they should have been visible on day one.

Also, the Genesis account clearly says that birds were created with sea creatures on day five while land animals were not created until day six. This is in direct opposition to the Darwinian view that birds evolved from land animals. The biblical account says that birds preceded land animals. The theistic evolutionist view says exactly the opposite.

One of the most unfortunate trends in modern Christianity is that of reinterpreting Genesis to accommodate evolutionary theories. Many well-known Bible teachers and apologists have caved in to the evolutionists and have come to believe that adhering to a literal interpretation of Genesis is somehow detrimental to the credibility of Christians. If anything, evolutionists lose respect for those whose belief in the Bible is so tenuous that they are willing to quickly compromise it. Although the number of true creationists may be dwindling in academia, several faithful organizations such as Answers in Genesis, the Creation Research Society, and the Institute for Creation Research have affirmed that the Bible is not only compatible with real science, but affirm that not a single word in the Bible has ever been disproved by true science. The Bible is God's living Word, given to us by the Creator of the universe, and His description of how He created that universe is not compatible with the theory of evolution, even a *"theistic"* understanding of evolution.

11. QUESTION:
"What is the Gap Theory? Did anything happen between Genesis 1:1 and 1:2?"

ANSWER: Genesis 1:1-2 states, *"In the beginning God created the heavens and the earth. Now the earth was formless and empty, darkness was over the surface of the deep, and the Spirit of God was hovering over the waters."* The Gap Theory is the view that God created a fully functional earth with all animals, including the dinosaurs and other creatures we know only from the fossil record. Then, the theory goes, something happened to destroy the earth completely—some speculate it was the fall of Satan to earth—so that the earth became without form and void. At this point, God started all over again, recreating the earth in its paradise form as further described in Genesis.

There are too many problems with this theory to describe adequately in a brief response, not the least of which is that if something important had occurred between the two verses, God would have told us so. God would not have left us to speculate in ignorance about such important events. Second, Genesis 1:31 says God declared His creation to be *"very good,"* which He certainly could not say if evil had already entered the world via Satan's fall in the *"gap."* Along the same line, if the fossil record is to be explained by the millions of years in the gap, that means death, disease, and suffering were common many ages before Adam fell. But the Bible tells us that it was Adam's sin that introduced death, disease, and suffering to all life: *"Sin entered the world through one man, and death through sin"* (Romans 5:12).

Those who hold to the Gap Theory do so in order to reconcile the theories of modern scientists who hold to the old-earth theory—the belief that the earth is billions of years older than can be accounted for by adding up the genealogies of man found in the Bible. Even well-meaning evangelicals have bought into the old-earth theory, handling much of Genesis 1 allegorically, while attempting to hold to a literal interpretation of the rest of Scripture. The danger in this is in determining at what point to stop allegorizing and begin interpreting literally. Was Adam a literal person? How do we know? If he was not, then did he really bring sin into the human race, or can we allegorize that as well? And if there was no literal Adam to introduce the sin which we all inherit, then there was no reason for Jesus to die on the cross. A non-literal original sin denies the reason for Christ's coming in the first place, as explained in 1 Corinthians 15:22: *"For as in Adam all die, even so in Christ all shall be made alive."* At that point, Christianity itself becomes a hoax and the Bible just a nice book of stories and fables. Can we not see where this type of *"reasoning"* gets us?

Genesis 1 simply cannot be reconciled with the notion that creation occurred over long periods of time, nor that these periods occurred in the space between Genesis 1:1 and 1:2. What took place between Genesis 1:1 and 1:2? Absolutely nothing! Genesis 1:1 tells us that God created the heavens and the earth. Genesis 1:2 informs us that when He first created the earth, it was formless, empty, and dark; it was not finished and not yet inhabited by creatures. The rest of Genesis chapter 1 tells us how God completed the formless, empty, and dark earth by filling it with life, beauty, and goodness. The Bible is true, literal, and perfect (Psalm 19:7-9). Science has never disproved anything in the Bible and it never will. The Bible is supreme truth and therefore is the standard by which scientific theory should be evaluated, not the other way around.

12. QUESTION:
"Was Noah's flood global or local?"

ANSWER: The biblical passages regarding the flood make it clear that it was global. Genesis 7:11 states that *"all the springs of the great deep burst forth, and the floodgates of the heavens were opened."* Genesis 1:6-7 and 2:6 tell us that the pre-flood environment was much different from that which we experience today. Based on these and other biblical descriptions, it is reasonably speculated that at one time the earth was covered by some kind of water canopy. This canopy could have been a vapor canopy, or it might have consisted of rings, somewhat like Saturn's ice rings. This, in combination with a layer of water underground, released upon the land (Genesis 2:6) would have resulted in a global flood.

The clearest verses that show the extent of the flood are Genesis 7:19-23. Regarding the waters, *"They rose greatly on the earth, and all the high mountains under the entire heavens were covered. The waters rose and covered the mountains to a depth of more than twenty feet. Every living thing that moved on the earth perished—birds, livestock, wild animals, all the creatures that swarm over the earth, and all mankind. Everything on dry land that had the breath of life in its nostrils died. Every living thing on the face of the earth was wiped out; men and animals and the creatures that move along the ground and the birds of the air were wiped from the earth. Only Noah was left, and those with him in the ark."*

In the above passage, we not only find the word "all" being used repeatedly, but we also find *"all the high mountains under the entire heavens were covered," "the waters rose and covered the mountains to a depth of more than twenty feet,"* and *"every living thing that moved on the earth perished."* These descriptions clearly describe a universal flood covering the whole earth. Also, if the flood was localized, why did God instruct Noah to build an ark instead of merely telling Noah to move and causing the animals to migrate? And why did He instruct Noah to build an ark large enough to house all of the different kinds of land animals found on the earth? If the flood was not global, there would have been no need for an ark.

Peter also describes the universality of the flood in 2 Peter 3:6-7, where he states, *"By these waters also the world of that time was deluged and destroyed. By the same word the present heavens and earth are reserved for fire, being kept for the day of judgment and destruction of ungodly men."* In these verses Peter compares the *"universal"* coming judgment to the flood of Noah's time and states that the world that existed then was flooded with water. Further, many biblical writers accepted the historicity of the worldwide flood (Isaiah 54:9; 1 Peter 3:20; 2 Peter 2:5; Hebrews 11:7). Lastly, the Lord Jesus Christ believed in the universal flood and took it as the type of the coming destruction of the world when He returns (Matthew 24:37-39; Luke 17:26-27).

There are many extra-biblical evidences that point to a worldwide catastrophe such as a global flood. There are vast fossil graveyards found on every continent and large amounts of coal deposits that would require the rapid covering of vast quantities of vegetation. Oceanic fossils are found upon mountain tops around the world. Cultures in all parts of the world have some form of flood legend. All of these facts and many others are evidence of a global flood.

13. QUESTION:
"What is the origin of the different races?"

ANSWER: The Bible does not explicitly give us the origin of the different *"races"* or skin colors in humanity. In actuality, there is only one race—the human race. Within the human race is diversity in skin color and other physical characteristics. Some speculate that when God confused the languages at the tower of Babel (Genesis 11:1-9), He also created racial diversity. It is possible that God made genetic changes to humanity to better enable people to survive in different ecologies, such as the darker skin of Africans being better equipped genetically to survive the excessive heat in Africa. According to this view, God confused the languages, causing humanity to segregate linguistically, and then created genetic racial differences based on where each racial group would eventually settle. While possible, there is no explicit biblical basis for this view. The races/skin colors of humanity are nowhere mentioned in connection with the tower of Babel.

After the flood, when the different languages came into existence, groups that spoke one language moved away with others of the same language. In doing so, the gene pool for a specific group shrank dramatically as the group no longer had the entire human population to mix with. Closer inbreeding took place, and in time certain features were emphasized in these different groups (all of which were present as a possibility in the genetic code). As further inbreeding occurred through the generations, the gene pool grew smaller and smaller, to the point that people of one language family all had the same or similar features.

Another explanation is that Adam and Eve possessed the genes to produce black, brown, and white offspring (and everything else in between). This would be similar to how a mixed-race couple sometimes has children that vary in color. Since God obviously desired humanity to be diverse in appearance, it makes sense that God would have given Adam and Eve the ability to produce children of different skin tones. Later, the only survivors of the flood were Noah and his wife, Noah's three sons and their wives—eight people in all (Genesis 7:13). Perhaps Noah's daughters-in-law were of different races. It is also possible that Noah's wife was of a different race than Noah. Maybe all eight of them were of mixed race, which would mean they possessed the genetics to produce children of different races. Whatever the explanation, the most important aspect of this question is that we are all the same race, all created by the same God, all created for the same purpose—to glorify Him.

14. QUESTION:
"Who was Lilith / Lillith? Does the Bible say anything about Adam having another wife before Eve?"

ANSWER: There are legends that Adam had a wife before Eve who was named Lilith, but this is not found in the Bible. The legends vary significantly, but they all essentially agree that Lilith left Adam because she did not want to submit to him. According to the legends, Lilith was an evil, wicked woman who committed adultery with Satan and produced a race of evil creatures. None of this is true. There is no biblical basis whatsoever for these concepts. There is no one in the Bible named Lilith.

The passage most often pointed to as evidence for Lilith is Isaiah 34:14, which in the NRSV reads, *"there too Lilith shall repose.*" This is a poor translation. Every other major translation of the Bible reads something to the effect of *"night creature"* or *"screech owl."* Even if *"demon monster named Lilith"* was the proper translation of the Hebrew word, Adam is nowhere even hinted at in this passage or its context. Whatever the Lilith was, it is not given any connection whatsoever to Adam or Creation.

Another commonly used support for Lilith is the differing Creation accounts in Genesis chapters 1-2. Some claim that the woman in Genesis 1 was Lilith, with the woman in Genesis 2 being Eve. This is completely ludicrous. Rather, Genesis chapter 2 is a "closer look" at the creation of Adam and Eve as recorded in Genesis chapter 1. The Bible specifically says that Adam and Eve were the first human beings ever created (Genesis 1:26-28; 2:18-25). This *"Lilith"* myth is popular in some radical feminist movements because Lilith is an example of a woman refusing to submit to male headship. While there are myths outside of the Word of God regarding Lilith, her complete absence from Scripture demonstrates that she is nothing more than a myth.

15. QUESTION:
"Did God use the "Big Bang" to create the universe?"

ANSWER: Some Christians are vehemently opposed to the *"Big Bang"* theory. They view it as an attempt to explain the origin of the universe apart from God. Others ascribe to the Big Bang theory, with the view that it was God Himself who caused the Big Bang. God, in His infinite wisdom and power, could have chosen to use a Big Bang method to create the universe, but He did not. The reason that can be absolutely stated is that the Bible argues against such a method. Here are some of the contradictions between the Bible and the Big Bang theory:

In Genesis 1, God created the earth before the sun and stars. The Big Bang theory requires it to be the other way around. In Genesis 1, God creates the earth, sun, moon, stars, plant life, animal life, and mankind in a span of six 24-hour days. The Big Bang theory requires billions of years. In Genesis 1, God created all matter by His spoken word. The Big Bang theory begins with matter already in existence and never explains the initial source or cause of matter.

In Genesis 1, God breathed life into the body of the perfectly created Adam. The Big Bang theory requires billions of years, and billions of chance circumstances, to get around to the first human, and it never can explain how the first microscopic life form happened to *"evolve"* from a non-living atom. In the Bible, God is eternal and the matter and the universe are not. There are different versions of the Big Bang theory, but in most of them the universe and/or matter is eternal. In Genesis 1, the existence of God is assumed, *"In the beginning God..."* The true purpose of the Big Bang theory is to deny His existence.

16. QUESTION:
"Why did God create such a vast universe and other planets if there is only life on Earth?"

ANSWER: The question of whether God created life on other planets is certainly fascinating. Psalm 19:1 says that *"the heavens declare the glory of God, and the firmament shows His handiwork."* Everything that God has made, be it you and me, or wildlife, or angels, or stars and planets, has been created for

His glory. When we see a breathtaking view of the Milky Way or peer at Saturn through a telescope, we are amazed at the wonders of God!

David wrote in Psalm 8:3, " *I consider Your heavens, the work of Your fingers, the moon and the stars, which You have ordained.* " When we see the vast number of stars, then read that scientists have discovered thousands upon thousands of galaxies, each containing millions of stars, we should be stand in reverent fear of a God so immense to make all that and call it the work of His fingers! Furthermore, Psalm 147:4 tells us that *"He counts the number of the stars, He calls them all by name."* It is impossible for mankind to know how many stars there are, not to mention the "name" of every star! *"Indeed My hand has laid the foundation of the earth, And My right hand has stretched out the heavens; When I call to them, They stand up together"* (Isaiah 48:13).

Space and planets were created for God's glory. We know that stars and planets outside our solar system exist, and these, too, were created for the glory of God. A constantly expanding universe is yet another conjecture that has yet to be proven. The next star farther than the sun is over 4 light-years away, and that isn't even a measurable fraction of the size of the known universe, expanding or not.

As to whether there is life on other planets, we simply do not know. So far, no evidence of life on the other planets of our solar system has been found. Considering the nearness of the end times, it is unlikely that man will progress far enough to visit other galaxies before the Lord's return. Wherever life exists or doesn't exist, God is still the Creator and Controller of all things, and all things were made for His glory.

17. QUESTION:
"How can the light of stars billions of light years away from the earth have reached us if the earth is only thousands of years old?"

ANSWER: Distant Starlight—A light-year is the maximum distance that light can travel in one year in the vacuum of space. Consequently, it takes billions of years for light to travel billions of light-years through space. From our vantage point here on

Earth we can see light from stars that are billions of light-years away. It is reasonable, therefore, to assume that our universe is at least billions of years old—old enough to give the light from these stars enough time to reach our planet billions of light-years away.

This reasonable assumption contradicts the Young Earth (YE) perspective, which claims that the universe is less than 10,000 years old. If there was not a strong scientific case for the YE perspective, this contradiction would not merit a second thought. The growing body of evidence supporting the YE view is substantial enough, however, to warrant a thoughtful investigation into whether or not this apparent contradiction can be resolved reasonably. And so we ask the question: How can the light of stars billions of light-years away reach the earth in only a few thousand years?

GRAVITATIONAL TIME DILATION

According to Albert Einstein, space is not the empty *"nothingness"* that most of us perceive it to be. It is filled with what Einstein called ether. Dictionary.com defines ether as *"an all-pervading, infinitely elastic, massless medium."* Everything that exists within the bounds of our universe does so within this massless medium.

As dictionary.com notes, ether is infinitely elastic. It can be stretched and distorted. In order to visualize this, imagine a tightly stretched cloth. This is ether. Now imagine dropping a heavy ball (like a bowling ball) onto the cloth, right in the middle. This would cause the cloth to sag in the middle. The heavy ball represents dense matter, like our planet. Einstein believed that matter causes space to sag, similar to how the heavy ball causes the stretched cloth to sag. These sags in space are known as gravity wells.

Now, if we placed smaller, lighter balls (like marbles) onto the cloth along with the heavy ball, they would roll toward the center, into the sag caused by the heavy ball. Moreover, they would contribute to the overall sagging of the cloth, even if only slightly. This motion towards the center represents gravity. According to Einstein's view of gravity, if smaller, lighter forms of matter are close enough, they can be drawn into the gravity wells of larger, denser forms of matter. While they each create their own sag in space, some gravity wells are deeper and more influential than others (that is, they generate a stronger gravitational force). One thing they all have in common: they distort time.

In the 1960s, physicists Robert Pound and Glen Rebka experimentally confirmed a theoretical consequence of Einstein's Theories of Relativity called the Gravitational Time Dilation Effect (GTDE). Pound and Rebka were able to demonstrate that time passes more slowly for objects the farther they travel into a gravity well. For example, Global Positioning System (GPS) satellites are farther away from the earth than objects on the planet's surface and are therefore less immersed in the gravity well caused by Earth's mass. The result is that time passes a little more quickly for our GPS satellites than it does for us here on the surface, since we are deeper inside of the earth's gravity well. Atomic clocks aboard the satellites and here on Earth have been used to detect and measure this difference in the rate of time's passage.

Likewise, an atomic clock in Greenwich, England (at sea level), records a slower rate of time than the atomic clock in Boulder, Colorado (at 5,430 feet above sea level). At these relatively small altitudinal differences, the measurable effect is minor. The effect across the greater cosmos can be much more dramatic. The deeper a gravity well, the stronger the GTDE. In fact, according to General Relativity, time actually stands still at the boundary of a black hole—an area known to scientists as an *"event horizon,"* where gravity is so intense that even light cannot escape (hence the name "black hole").

Now, let's set aside the GTDE for a moment and consider another important astronomical phenomenon: stellar redshifts. Redshifts are a Doppler effect phenomenon whereby radiational wavelengths (like those of starlight) lengthen as they move farther away from an observer. The general consensus among astronomers is that observed stellar redshifts indicate that the universe is expanding (Hubble's Law). By extrapolating this expansion backwards, it becomes apparent that the primordial universe was somewhat denser, more compact than it is today.

In a bounded universe wherein matter has a center and an edge, the material compression as described above would serve to deepen the gravity well caused by the combined mass of the universe. This would intensify the GTDE, causing time to pass much more slowly near the center of the universe (deeper in the well) than near its edge (nearer the surface of the well).

The implication is paradoxical: even if the entire universe was created all at once in the beginning (and should therefore be the same age), some parts can be substantially younger than others due to the relativistic nature of time. Light could travel billions of light-years over billions of years in some parts of the universe in what we on Earth would perceive to be a much shorter period of time. As the universe expands and matter spreads out across space, the universal gravity well would gradually even out, lessening the rate of time difference across the universe.

Many astrophysicists and astronomers reject the idea of a bounded universe with our galaxy, the Milky Way, near or at its center. But this is a philosophical presupposition, not a scientific conclusion founded upon empirical data. As world-renowned astrophysicist Dr. George F. R. Ellis candidly explained, *"People need to be aware that there is a range of models that could explain the observations. For instance, I can construct you a spherically symmetrical universe with Earth at its center, and you cannot disprove it based on observations... you can only exclude it on philosophical grounds. In my view there is absolutely nothing wrong in that. What I want to bring into the open is the fact that we are using philosophical criteria in choosing our models. A lot of cosmology tries to hide that."* (W. Wayt Gibbs, *"Profile: George F. R. Ellis,"* Scientific American, October 1995, Vol. 273, No.4, p. 55)

In summary, the Gravitational Time Dilation Effect is a theoretical solution to the YE problem of distant starlight which, amazingly, reconciles evidence for a young Earth with evidence for an old universe. Many astrophysicists and astronomers reject one of the major foundational suppositions upon which the GTDE explanation rests (a bounded universe with the Milky Way at or near the center), not because of the observable data but because of their philosophical perspectives.

18. QUESTION: *"What is the location of the Garden of Eden?"*

ANSWER: The only thing the Bible tells us concerning the Garden of Eden's location is found in Genesis 2:10-14, *"A river watering the garden flowed from Eden; from there it was separated into four headwaters. The name of the first is the Pishon; it winds*

through the entire land of Havilah, where there is gold... The name
of the second river is the Gihon; it winds through the entire land
of Cush. The name of the third river is the Tigris; it runs along the
east side of Asshur. And the fourth river is the Euphrates." The
exact identities of the Pishon and Gihon Rivers is unknown, but
the Tigris and Euphrates Rivers are well known.

If the Tigris and Euphrates mentioned are the same rivers
by those names today, that would put the Garden of Eden
somewhere in the Middle East, likely in Iraq. It cannot be mere
coincidence that the Middle East region is where the planet was
most lush—the place where the Garden of Eden was. If oil is, as
most scientists believe, primarily decayed vegetation and animal
matter, then this is the area where we might expect to find the
greatest deposits of oil. Since the Garden was the epitome of
perfection, it stands to reason that the decomposition of the
earth's most perfect and lush organic materials would produce
vast stores of the earth's best oil.

People have searched for the Garden of Eden for centuries
to no avail. There are various locations that people claim as
the original location of the Garden of Eden, but we cannot be
sure. What happened to the Garden of Eden? The Bible does

not specifically say. It is likely that the Garden of Eden was completely destroyed in the Flood or that it lies decomposing into oil buried beneath centuries of sand deposits.

19. QUESTION: "What does the Bible say about dragons?"

ANSWER: The Bible mentions a dragon in Revelation chapters 12, 13, 16, and 20. Revelation 20:2 identifies the dragon: *"He seized the dragon, that ancient serpent, who is the devil, or Satan, and bound him for a thousand years."* The Bible is not teaching that dragons ever truly existed. Rather, it is only comparing Satan to a fire-breathing monster.

It is very interesting to note, however, that nearly every major ancient culture has myths and legends about giant reptiles. How would these civilizations, continents and millennia apart, all come up with legends of giant reptile creatures? Evolutionary scientists tell us that dinosaurs existed millions of years before human beings. Dinosaur fossils were not discovered until thousands of years after the myths of giants reptiles began. How can this be?

The Bible mentions two creatures that seem remarkably similar to the dinosaurs, the leviathan and behemoth, in Job chapters 40-41. It is the view of creation scientists that all the *"dragon"* myths came from real contact between human beings and dinosaurs. The Bible tells us that all animals were created around 6000 years ago and co-existed with human beings. That would explain how all human cultures have myths about giant reptiles—because they actually saw them! The *"fire-breathing"* aspect of a dragon is possibly a myth (although there have been some interesting discoveries), but the universal legends of giant reptiles point to real contact between human beings and dinosaurs.

20. QUESTION: *"What happened at the Tower of Babel?"*

ANSWER: The Tower of Babel is described in Genesis 11:1-9. After the Flood, God commanded humanity to *"increase in number and fill the earth"* (Genesis 9:1). Humanity decided to do the exact opposite, *"Then they said, 'Come, let us build ourselves a city, with a tower that reaches to the heavens, so that we may make a name for ourselves and not be scattered over the face of the whole earth"* (Genesis 11:4). Humanity decided to build a great city and all congregate there. They decided to build a gigantic tower as a symbol of their power, to make a name for themselves (Genesis 11:4). This tower is remembered as the Tower of Babel.

In response, God confused the languages of humanity so that they could no longer communicate with each other (Genesis 11:7). The result was that people congregated with other people who spoke the same language, and then went together and settled in other parts of the world (Genesis 11:8-9). God confused the languages at the Tower of Babel to enforce His command for humanity to spread throughout the entire world.

Some Bible teachers also believe that God created the different races of humanity at the Tower of Babel. This is possible, but it is not taught in the biblical text. It seems more likely that the different races existed prior to the Tower of Babel and that God confused the languages at least partially based on the different races. From the Tower of Babel, humanity divided based on language (and possibly race) and settled in various parts of the world.

Genesis 10:5, 20 and 31 describe Noah's descendants spreading out over the earth *"by their clans and languages, in their territories and nations."* How is this possible since God did not confuse the languages until the Tower of Babel in Genesis chapter 11? Genesis 10 lists the descendants of Noah's three sons: Shem, Ham, and Japheth. It lists their descendants for several generations. With the long life spans of that time (see Genesis 11:10-25), the genealogies in Genesis 10 likely cover several hundreds of years. The Tower of Babel account, told in Genesis 11:1-9, is a *"flashback"* to the point in Genesis 10 when the languages were confused. Genesis 10 tells us of different languages. Genesis 11 tells us how the different languages originated.

21. QUESTION:
"Did God create other people in addition to Adam and Eve?"

ANSWER: There is no indication anywhere in the Bible that God created any humans other than Adam and Eve. In Genesis 2 we read, *"This is the account of the heavens and the earth when they were created, in the day that the LORD God made earth and heaven. Now no shrub of the field was yet in the earth, and no plant of the field had yet sprouted, for the LORD God had not sent rain upon the earth, and there was no man to cultivate the ground. But a mist used to rise from the earth and water the whole surface of the ground. Then the LORD God formed man of dust from the ground, and breathed into his nostrils the breath of life; and man became a living being. The LORD God planted a garden toward the east, in Eden; and there He placed the man whom He had formed... Then the LORD God said, 'It is not good for the man to be alone; I will make him a helper suitable for him.' ...So the LORD God caused a deep sleep to fall upon the man, and he slept; then He took one of his ribs and closed up the flesh at that place. The LORD God fashioned into a woman the rib which He had taken from the man, and brought her to the man"* (Genesis 2:4-8, 18, 21-22).

Notice that the passage says, *"There He placed the man whom He had formed."* Not the *"men,"* just the one *"man."* And this man was alone (v. 18) so God made a woman out of his rib to be his companion. All other human beings have descended from these two original people. The two main reasons why this question usually comes up are (1) Cain's wife, and (2) the origin of the different races. If the only people on the earth were children of Adam and Eve, whom did Cain marry and how did we get all the different races of people with their different skin colors from just two people? For answers to these issues, please read *"Who was Cain's wife?"* and *"What is the origin of the different races?"*

22. QUESTION:
"Had it ever rained before the Flood in Noah's day?"

ANSWER: Some interpret Hebrews 11:7 as saying it had never rained prior to the Flood: *"By faith Noah, when warned about things not yet seen, in holy fear built an ark to save his family. By his faith he condemned the world and became heir of the righteousness* *that comes by faith."* Rain could be the correct understanding of *"things not yet seen,"* or it could be referring to the Flood in general.

Genesis 2:6 says, *"But streams came up from the earth and watered the whole surface of the ground."* Before the Flood (Genesis chapters 6-9), the earth was surrounded by a *"firmament"* or canopy of water, creating almost a greenhouse effect on the earth's climate. These are the waters that God released, causing the Flood. It seems that before the Flood the dew and ample water supply were enough to keep creation watered. The Bible does not specifically tell us whether or not it had rained before the Flood. Noah seemed to understand what rain was when God mentioned it to him (Genesis 7:4-5). Genesis 2:4-6 mentions that God did not send rain on the earth until after He created Adam and Eve. We can speculate that it had rained before the Flood, but, again, the Bible does not specifically say.

23. QUESTION:
"Did the Bible copy the Flood account from other myths and legends?"

ANSWER: It is true that the Genesis flood account shares many striking similarities with the Babylonian Gilgamesh epic, and with the Babylonian Atrahasis epic, for that matter. In fact, literally hundreds of flood traditions have been preserved all over the world, with traditions abounding in Europe, Asia, Africa, and Australia, as well as both of the Americas, and the Genesis account shares similarities with most of them. Of the flood traditions which have survived to the present time, about 95% describe a global cataclysmic deluge, 88% tell of a favored family of humans saved from drowning to reestablish the human race after the deluge, 66% say the family was forewarned of the coming cataclysm, 66% blame the wickedness of man for the deluge, and 70% record a boat as being the means by which the chosen family (and animals) survived the flood. More than one third of these traditions mention birds being sent out from the boat.

Since every culture has descended directly from the flood's survivors, it is logical that stories of this traumatic event are both abundant and universal, having been passed down from generation to generation. This is certainly the case. Many of these traditions are remarkably consistent, considering the relative isolation of the cultures, the length of time that has elapsed since the flood, and the human tendency to embellish, exaggerate, and distort stories over time. The Babylonian and biblical accounts of the flood appear to represent different retellings of an essentially identical flood tradition.

Skeptics want to imagine that there was, in fact, no flood and that the Bible's flood account was borrowed from a Babylonian myth. The evidence seems to suggest otherwise: there was, in fact, a catastrophic worldwide deluge, and the veracity of the biblical account is attested to by numerous other similar ancient accounts. In addition to abundant historical evidence, there is a wealth of physical proof in favor of the flood's historicity. The flood of Noah's day was most certainly a real historical event, and the biblical account of what happened is trustworthy.

24. QUESTION:
"What is the Intelligent Design Theory?"

ANSWER: The Intelligent Design Theory says that intelligent causes are necessary to explain the complex, information-rich structures of biology and that these causes are empirically detectable. Certain biological features defy the standard Darwinian random-chance explanation, because they appear to have been designed. Since design logically necessitates an intelligent designer, the appearance of design is cited as evidence for a designer. There are three primary arguments in the Intelligent Design Theory: 1) irreducible complexity, 2) specified complexity, and 3) the anthropic principle.

Irreducible complexity is defined as *"...a single system which is composed of several well-matched interacting parts that contribute to the basic function, wherein the removal of any one of the parts causes the system to effectively cease functioning."* Simply put, life is comprised of intertwined parts that rely on each other in order to be useful. Random mutation may account for the development of a new part, but it cannot account for the concurrent development of multiple parts necessary for a functioning system. For example, the human eye is obviously a very useful system. Without the eyeball, the optic nerve, and the visual cortex, a randomly mutated incomplete eye would actually be counterproductive to the survival of a species and would therefore be eliminated through the process of natural selection. An eye is not a useful system unless all its parts are present and functioning properly at the same time.

Specified complexity is the concept that, since specified complex patterns can be found in organisms, some form of guidance must have accounted for their origin. The specified complexity argument states that it is impossible for complex patterns to be developed through random processes. For example, a room filled with 100 monkeys and 100 computers may eventually produce a few words, or maybe even a sentence, but it would never produce a Shakespearean play. And how much more complex is biological life than a Shakespearean play?

The anthropic principle states that the world and universe are *"fine-tuned"* to allow for life on earth. If the ratio of elements in the air of the earth was altered slightly, many species would very quickly cease to exist. If the earth were a few miles closer or further away from the sun, many species would cease to exist. The existence and development of life on earth requires so many variables to be perfectly in tune that it would be impossible for all the variables to come into being through random, uncoordinated events.

While the Intelligent Design Theory does not presume to identify the source of intelligence (whether it be God or UFOs or something else), the vast majority of Intelligent Design theorists are theists. They see the appearance of design which pervades the biological world as evidence for the existence of God. There are, however, a few atheists who cannot deny the strong evidence for design, but are not willing to acknowledge a Creator God. They tend to interpret the data as evidence that earth was seeded by some sort of master race of extraterrestrial creatures (aliens). Of course, they do not address the origin of the aliens either, so they are back to the original argument with no credible answer.

The Intelligent Design Theory is not biblical creationism. There is an important distinction between the two positions. Biblical creationists begin with a conclusion that the biblical account of creation is reliable and correct, that life on Earth was designed by an intelligent agent—God. They then look for evidence from the natural realm to support this conclusion. Intelligent Design theorists begin with the natural realm and reach the conclusion that life on Earth was designed by an intelligent agent (whoever that might be).

25. QUESTION: *"What was God doing before He created the universe?"*

ANSWER: Our finite minds find it hard to comprehend that before the universe was created, God existed alone. We know from John 1:1 that Jesus also existed: *"In the beginning was the Word and the Word was with God, and the Word was God. The preincarnate Christ was intimately united with the Father, so as to partake of His glory and to be appropriately called God."* He has Himself explained it in John 17:5: *"And now Father, glorify Me with Yourself with the glory which I had with You before the world was."*

We also know that the Holy Spirit was present before we

were created. Genesis 1:1 describes the Spirit *"hovering over the face"* of the dark and formless earth. So, before time even existed, God existed in three Persons: Father, Son and Holy Spirit. The Trinity existed in perfect harmony and flawlessness, having all they needed in one another. David said in Psalms 16:11 that "joy and pleasures forever more" are in the presence of God. That means to be in the presence of God carries with it an overwhelming sense of joy, fulfillment, and pleasure. Before creation, God felt complete joy and fulfillment as He perfectly beheld and communed with Himself. God has and always will experience complete joy because He has complete and perfect knowledge of Himself.

So before He created the universe, God experienced absolute satisfaction in Himself. God dwelt joyfully alone in eternity as the Trinity. These three were together in fellowship with one another from all eternity. They loved each other. We know at some point they discussed the redemption of mankind (Ephesians 1:4-5; 2 Timothy 1:9; John 17:24), but everything else lies in mystery.

26. QUESTION: "What does Creation 'ex nihilo' mean?"

ANSWER: *"Ex nihilo"* is Latin for *"from nothing."* The term *"creation ex nihilo"* refers to God creating everything from nothing. In the beginning, God created the heavens and the earth (Genesis 1:1). Prior to that moment there was nothing. God didn't make the universe from preexisting building blocks. He started from scratch.

The Bible never expressly states that God made everything from nothing, but it is implied. In Hebrews 11:3 we read, "By faith we understand that the worlds were framed by the word of God, so that the things which are seen were not made of things which are visible." Scholars take this to mean that the universe came into existence by divine command and was not assembled from preexisting matter or energy.

Humans can be very creative, but we require materials from which to build something. God is not so constrained. This is difficult for us to comprehend because of a fundamental law of physics which we are all familiar with. Whether or not we know what it's called, we're all familiar with a very basic principle. The *"first law of science"* states that matter (the stuff the universe is made of) cannot be created or destroyed. Matter can be converted from solid to liquid to gas to plasma and back again; atoms can be combined into molecules and split into their component parts; but matter cannot be created from nothing or completely destroyed. And so this idea that God created everything from nothing is not natural to us. It's not natural at all—it's supernatural.

The term *"creation ex nihilo"* refers to the supernatural event which was the beginning of the universe. It was the moment that God created something from nothing.

27. QUESTION:
"How did Noah fit all the animals on the Ark?"

ANSWER: How did Noah fit all of those animals on the ark? Was the ark big enough to fit *"two of every kind… of the birds after their kind, and of the animals after their kind, of* *every creeping thing of the ground after its kind,"* and seven of some kinds? What about food? There had to be enough room to store enough food to last Noah and his family (8 in all), plus all of the animals, at least a year (see Genesis 7:11; 8:13-18) and maybe more, depending on how long it took for vegetation to grow back. That's a lot of food! What about drinking water? Is it realistic to believe that Noah's boat was big enough to store all of these animals and all of this food and water for over a year?

The dimensions for the ark given in Genesis are 300 cubits long, 50 cubits wide and 30 cubits high (Genesis 6:15). What is a cubit? A cubit is an ancient unit of measurement, the length of the forearm from the elbow to the longest finger (the term *"cubit"* comes from the Latin word *"cubitum"* which means *"elbow."* The Hebrew word for *"cubit"* is *"ammah."* As everybody's arms are different lengths, this unit may seem a bit ambiguous to some, but scholars generally agree that it represents somewhere between 17 and 22 inches (43-56 centimeters). The ancient Egyptian cubit is known to have been 21.888 inches. So, doing the math,

300 x 22 inches = 6,600; 50 x 22 inches = 1,100;

30 x 22 inches = 660

6,600/12 = 550 feet; 1100/12 = 91.7 feet; 660/12 = 55 feet.

Thus, the ark could have been up to 550 feet long, 91.7 feet wide and 55 feet high. These are not unreasonable dimensions. But how much storage space does this amount to? Well, 550 x 91.7 x 55 = 2,773,925 cubic feet. (If we take the smallest measurement of cubit, 17 inches, we end up with 1,278,825 cubic feet). Of course, not all of it would have been free space. The ark had three levels (Genesis 6:16) and a lot of rooms (Genesis 6:14), the walls of which would have taken up space. Nevertheless, it has been calculated that a little more than half (54.75%) of the 2,773,925 cubic feet could store 125,000 sheep-sized animals, leaving over 1.5 million cubic feet of free space

John Woodmorappe, author of the definitive Noah's Ark: A Feasibility Study, estimated that only about 15% of the animals on the ark would have been larger than a sheep. This figure does not take into account the possibility that God may have brought Noah *"infant"* animals, which can be significantly smaller than adult animals.

How many animals were on the ark? Woodmorappe estimates about 16,000 *"kinds."* What is a *"kind"*? The designation of "kind" is thought to be much broader than the designation *"species."* Even as there are over 400 dog breeds all belonging to one species (Canis familiaris), so many species can belong to one kind. Some think that the designation *"genus"* may be somewhat close to the biblical *"kind."*

Nevertheless, even if we presume that *"kind"* is synonymous with *"species,"* "there are not very many species of mammals, birds, amphibians and reptiles. The leading systematic biologist, Ernst Mayr, gives the number as 17,600. Allowing for two of each species on the ark, plus seven of the few so-called *"clean"* kinds of animals, plus a reasonable increment for known extinct species, it is obvious that not more than, say, 50,000 animals were on the ark" (Morris, 1987).

Some have estimated that there were as many as 25,000 kinds of animals represented on the ark. This is a high-end estimation. With two of each kind and seven of some, the number of animals would exceed 50,000, though not by very much, relatively speaking. Regardless, whether there were 16,000 or 25,000 kinds of animals, even with two of each and seven of some, scholars agree that there was plenty of room for all of the animals on the ark, plus food and water with room to spare.

What about all of the excrement produced by all of these animals? How did 8 people manage to feed all of those animals and deal with tons of excrement on a daily basis? What about animals with specialized diet? How did plant-life survive? What about insects? There are a thousand other questions like these which could be raised, and they are all good questions. In the minds of many, these questions are unanswerable. But they are certainly nothing new. They have been asked over and over for centuries. And in all of that time researchers have sought answers. There are now numerous, very scholarly feasibility studies which have put Noah and his ark to the test.

With over 1,200 scholarly references to academic studies, Woodmorappe's book is *"a modern systematic evaluation of the alleged difficulties surrounding Noah's Ark"* (John Woodmorappe, *"A Resource for Answering the Critics of Noah's Ark,"* Impact No. 273, March 1996. Institute for Creation Research, 30 January 2005. Woodmorappe claims that after years of systematically examining all of the questions which have been raised, *"all of the arguments against the Ark are... found wanting. In fact, the vast majority of the anti-Ark arguments, at first superficially plausible, turn out to be easily invalidated."*

28. Question:
"Why did God put the tree of knowledge of good and evil in the Garden of Eden?"

Answer: God put the tree of knowledge of good and evil in the Garden of Eden to give Adam and Eve a choice to obey Him or disobey Him. Adam and Eve were free to do anything they wanted, except eat from the tree of knowledge of good and evil. Genesis 2:16-17, *"And the LORD God commanded the man, 'You are free to eat from any tree in the garden; but you must not eat from the tree of the knowledge of good and evil, for when you eat of it you will surely die.'"* If God had not given Adam and Eve the choice, they would have essentially been robots, simply doing what they were programmed to do. God created Adam and Eve to be *"free"* beings, able to make decisions, able to choose between good and evil. In order for Adam and Eve to truly be free, they had to have a choice.

There was nothing essentially evil about the tree or the fruit of the tree. It is unlikely that eating the fruit truly gave Adam and Eve any further knowledge. It was the act of disobedience that opened Adam and Eve's eyes to evil. Their sin of disobeying

God brought sin and evil into the world and into their lives. Eating the fruit, as an act of disobedience against God, was what gave Adam and Eve knowledge of evil (Genesis 3:6-7).

God did not want Adam and Eve to sin. God knew ahead of time what the results of sin would be. God knew that Adam and Eve would sin and would thereby bring evil, suffering, and death into the world. Why, then, did God allow Satan to tempt Adam and Eve? God allowed Satan to tempt Adam and Eve to force them to make the choice. Adam and Eve chose, of their own free will, to disobey God and eat the forbidden fruit. The results—evil, sin, suffering, sickness, and death—have plagued the world ever since. Adam and Eve's decision results in every person being born with a sin nature, a tendency to sin. Adam and Eve's decision is what ultimately required Jesus Christ to die on the cross and shed His blood on our behalf. Through faith in Christ, we can be free from sin's consequences, and ultimately free from sin itself. May we echo the words of the Apostle Paul in Romans 7:24-25, *"What a wretched man I am! Who will rescue me from this body of death? Thanks be to God—through Jesus Christ our Lord!"*

29. QUESTION:
"How could there be light on the first day of Creation if the sun was not created until the fourth day?"

ANSWER: The question of how there could be light on the first day of Creation when the sun was not created until the fourth day is a common one. Genesis 1:3-5 declares, *"And God said, 'Let there be light,' and there was light. God saw that the light was good, and He separated the light from the darkness. God called the light 'day,' and the darkness He called 'night.' And there was evening, and there was morning — the first day."* A few verses later we are informed, *"And God said, 'Let there be lights in the expanse of the sky to separate the day from the night, and let them serve as signs to mark seasons and days and years, and let them be lights in the expanse of the sky to give light on the earth.' And it was so. God made two great lights — the greater light to govern the day and the lesser light to govern the night. He also made the stars. God set them in the expanse of the sky to give light on the earth, to govern the day and the night, and to separate light from darkness. And God saw that it was good. And there was evening, and there was morning — the fourth day"* (Genesis 1:14-19). How can this be? How could there be light, mornings and evenings on the first, second, and third days if the sun, moon, and stars were not created until the fourth day?

This is only a problem if we fail to take into account an infinite and omnipotent God. God does not need the sun, moon, and stars to provide light. God is light! First John 1:5 declares, *"This is the message we have heard from him and declare to you: God is light; in Him there is no darkness at all."* God Himself was the light for the first three days of Creation, just as He will be in the new heavens and new earth, *"There will be no more night. They will not need the light of a lamp or the light of the sun, for the Lord God will give them light. And they will reign for ever and ever"* (Revelation 22:5). Until He created the sun, moon, and stars, God miraculously provided light during the *"day"* and may have done so during the *"night"* as well (Genesis 1:14).

Jesus said, *"I am the light of the world. Whoever follows me will never walk in darkness, but will have the light of life"* (John 8:12). Much more important than the light of day and night is the Light who provides eternal life to all who believe in Him. Those who do not believe in Him will be doomed to *"outer darkness where there is weeping and gnashing of teeth"* (Matthew 8:12).

30. QUESTION:
"What does the Bible say about the ice age?"

ANSWER: The Bible doesn't explicitly mention the Ice Age. It wasn't something that had much impact upon the writers of the Bible as they all lived in the Middle East, a region far south of the continental glaciations.

Creationists are typically delighted by evidence for an Ice Age. They contend that secular dating assumptions are off quite a bit, and they cite the Ice Age as an effect of the Flood. Secular scientists, on the other hand, have difficulty explaining how the Ice Age began. As Dr. Walt Brown points out, "An ice age implies extreme snowfall which, in turn, requires cold temperatures and heavy precipitation. Heavy precipitation can occur only if oceans are warm enough to produce equally heavy evaporation. How could warm oceans exist with cold atmospheric temperatures? Another problem is stopping an ice age once it begins—or beginning a new ice age after one ends. As glaciers expand, they reflect more of the sun's radiation away from Earth, lowering temperatures and causing glaciers to grow even more. Eventually the entire globe should freeze.

Conversely, if glaciers shrink, as they have in recent decades, the earth should reflect less heat into space, warm up, and melt all glaciers forever" (Walt Brown, In the Beginning, 2001, p 92).

31. QUESTION:
"How long did it take Noah to build the ark? How long was Noah on the ark?"

ANSWER: HOW LONG DID IT TAKE NOAH TO BUILD THE ARK? The Bible does not specifically say how long it took Noah to build the ark. When Noah is first mentioned in Genesis 5:32, he is 500 years old. When Noah enters the ark, he is 600 years old. The time it took to build the ark would depend on how much time had passed between Genesis 5:32 and the time that God commanded Noah to build the ark (Genesis 6:14-21). At the absolute most, it took 100 years.

HOW LONG WAS NOAH ON THE ARK? Noah entered the ark in the 600th year of his life, on the 17th day of the 2nd month (Genesis 7:11-13). Noah left the ark on the 27th day of the 2nd month of the following year (Genesis 8:14-15). Therefore, assuming a lunar calendar of 360 days, Noah was on the ark for approximately 370 days.

HOW MANY OF EACH TYPE OF ANIMAL DID NOAH TAKE ON THE ARK? Seven pairs of each kind of clean animal and two pairs of each kind of other animals were taken on the ark (Genesis 6:19-20; 7:2-3). By *"clean"* the Bible means animals that were "acceptable for sacrifice." That is why seven pairs of the clean animals were taken—so some of them could be sacrificed after the Flood was over without endangering the species.

HOW MANY PEOPLE WERE ON NOAH'S ARK? According to Genesis chapters 6-8, Noah, his wife, Noah's three sons (Shem, Ham, and Japheth), and their wives were on the ark. Therefore, there were eight people on the ark.

WHO WAS NOAH'S WIFE? The Bible nowhere specifically gives us the name or identity of Noah's wife. There is a tradition that she was Naamah (Genesis 4:22). While possible, this is not explicitly taught in the Bible.

32. QUESTION:
"Were Adam and Eve saved? How many children did Adam and Eve have? When were Adam and Eve created?"

WERE ADAM AND EVE SAVED? The Bible does not specifically tell us whether Adam and Eve were saved. Adam and Eve were the only two human beings who knew about God before they became tainted with sin. As a result, they likely still knew God better after their fall than any of us do today. Adam and Eve most definitely believed in and depended on God. God continued to talk with Adam and Eve and provide for them after the fall. Adam and Eve knew of God's promise that He would provide a Savior (Genesis 3:15). God made garments of skin for Adam and Eve after the fall (Genesis 3:21). Many scholars understand this as the first animal sacrifice, foreshadowing the eventual death of Christ on the cross for the sins of the world. Putting these facts together, it would seem that Adam and Eve were saved and did indeed go to heaven / paradise when they died.

HOW MANY CHILDREN DID ADAM AND EVE HAVE? The Bible does not give us a specific number. Adam and Eve had

Cain (Genesis 4:1), Abel (Genesis 4:2), Seth (Genesis 4:25), and many other sons and daughters (Genesis 5:4). With likely hundreds of years of child-bearing capability, Adam and Eve likely had 50+ children in their lifetime.

WHEN WERE ADAM AND EVE CREATED? If Old Testament history and the ages in Genesis chapter 5 are traced, Adam and Eve were likely created in approximately 4000 B.C.

WERE ADAM AND EVE CAVEMEN? Genesis chapter 3 records Adam and Eve having a fully intelligent conversation with God. Adam and Eve were surely *"primitive"* in their understanding of many concepts, but they were not *"ape-like"* or intellectually deficient by any means. Adam and Eve were the most perfect human beings in the history of the world.

HOW LONG WERE ADAM AND EVE IN THE GARDEN OF EDEN BEFORE THEY SINNED? The Bible does not explicitly tell us how long Adam and Eve were in the Garden of Eden before they sinned. It seems as if they were in the Garden for a short amount of time, possibly as little as a day or two. Adam and Eve did not conceive any children until after the Fall (Genesis 4:1-2), so it is unlikely they were in the Garden for very long.

DID ADAM AND EVE HAVE BELLYBUTTONS / NAVELS? A bellybutton is formed by the umbilical cord that connects a baby in the womb to its mother. Adam and Eve were created directly by God, and did not go through the normal birthing process. So, Adam and Eve would probably not have had bellybuttons.

33. QUESTION:
"Does the Bible say anything about a pre-Adamic race?"

ANSWER: The concept of a pre-Adamic race is the idea that God created a race of humans who lived on the Earth before He created Adam, the first man. This hypothesis has been promoted by various scholars at various times throughout history. Roman Emperor Julian the Apostate (circa A.D. 331–363) and Calvinist theologian Isaac de La Peyrère (1596-1676) are two notable examples.

We will look at two popular facets of the Preadamite Hypothesis: the hypothesis as it was proposed by Isaac de La Peyrère and the form which it takes in the *"Gap Theory"* (also known as the Ruin-Reconstruction interpretation). According to La Peyrère, God created the Gentiles on the sixth day when He said, "Let us make man in our image" (Genesis 1:26). He did not create the Jews until after the seventh day, His day of rest. At some point after the seventh day, God created Adam, the father of the Jews.

La Peyrère cited Scripture to support his hypothesis. Cain's fear of being lynched, his marriage to an unknown woman and the fact that he founded a city (Genesis 4:14-17) are all interpreted as evidence that another race of men coexisted with Adam and his family.

La Peyrère subsequently reinterpreted other passages of Scripture in light of his peculiar understanding of the Genesis account. Consider a very familiar passage, Romans 5:12-14: *"Therefore, just as through one man sin entered into the world, and death through sin, and so death spread to all men, because all sinned—for until the Law sin was in the world, but sin is not imputed when there is no law. Nevertheless death reigned from Adam until Moses, even over those who had not sinned in the likeness of the offense of Adam, who is a type of Him who was to come."*

This passage is traditionally interpreted as meaning that death began with Adam's sin and reigned unchecked among men (even among those who haven't actually eaten the forbidden fruit, those who have sinned but not *"in the likeness of the offense of Adam"*) until the Law was given to Moses. La Peyrère interpreted this passage another way. According to La Peyrère, the pre-Adamic Gentiles sinned against God, but in a manner less egregious than Adam (which is why Adam's sin brought death while theirs didn't). They merely sinned against God's moral will, while Adam sinned against His Law. Adam disobeyed God's prohibition by eating the forbidden fruit. He broke what La Peyrère called the Law of Paradise. Thus, according to La Peyrère, the pre-Adamic Gentiles were those who *"had not sinned in the likeness of the offense of Adam."*

By now it's obvious how misinterpreting one or two passages of Scripture can lead to all kinds of warped perceptions. The Scriptural problems with La Peyrère's interpretations are numerous.

First, Adam is called the *"first man"* (1 Corinthians 15:45). This is inconsistent with the idea that God created men before Adam. Second, according to La Peyrère, the Gentiles were to live outside of the Garden of Eden while Adam enjoyed paradise (a privilege which came with the responsibility of obeying the Law of Paradise—not eating the forbidden fruit). Genesis 2:5-8, however, says quite plainly that before God created "the man whom He had formed," the very same man which He placed in the garden, there were no men upon the earth to cultivate the ground. Third, God created Eve for Adam because he was alone, there was no one else like him around (*"It is not good for the man to be alone... but for Adam there was not found a helper suitable for him"* Genesis 2:18, 20). Fourth, Adam named his wife *"Eve"* *"because she was the mother of all the living"* (Genesis 3:20). The list goes on, but these passages should suffice to refute La Peyrère's misinterpretation.

As for Cain's fear of being lynched, his marriage to an unknown woman and the fact that he founded a city (Genesis 4:14-17), Adam was almost 130 years old by the time that Cain killed Abel (Adam had Seth, his next son after Abel's death, when he was about 130 years old; Genesis 4:25; 5:3). And we know that Adam had sons and daughters (Genesis 5:3). At 130 he could have had grandkids and great-grandkids by the time that Cain killed Abel. Cain had plenty of family members to be afraid of after killing his brother.

Cain apparently married a family member (a necessity back then) at some point before Abel's murder. It seems odd to us today, but incest wasn't outlawed by God until the Law of Moses. It may have been around that time that generations of degenerative genetic mutations began to take a toll on our DNA. God outlawed incest for our protection. It became (and remains) dangerous for close relatives to procreate because of shared genetic defects which become expressed in their children causing severe deformities and other problems.

As for Cain founding a city, if he lived to be the average age back then, he probably lived to be about 900 years old. By the time he died, his family would have been a small city. If Cain had a child at the age of 30, and his child had a child at the age of 30 and so on, Cain could have produced 30 generations by the time he died (30 generations times 30 years each equals 900 years).

The Ruin-Reconstruction interpretation takes a somewhat different approach to the pre-Adamic race theory. According to the Gap Theory, an unspecified amount of time passed between Genesis 1:1 and 1:2, during which God created a pre-Adamic race of men who lived upon the earth until God destroyed them in judgment. Other extinct creatures, like the dinosaurs, are said to have also lived during this time. Afterwards, the theory goes, God remodeled the earth in six days. He created Adam on the sixth day, and the rest is history. Some say that Satan's fall occurred at some point during the ambiguous gap.

A *"mistranslation"* has contributed to the case for this misinterpretation. In the King James Version of the Bible, God says to Adam, "Be fruitful, and multiply, and replenish the earth." Proponents of the Gap Theory emphasize the word *"replenish."* They interpret the text as saying that Adam and Eve were to refill the Earth. They were to fill it again. The problem with this view is that, regardless of what it says in English translations, the Hebrew word is mâlê', and it simply means *"to fill"* or *"to be full."* Moreover, the English translators of the King James Version knew the word means "to fill." They chose *"replenish"* because, in 17th-century Elizabethan English, *"replenish"* meant *"to fill"* (similar to how in modern English the word *"replete"* doesn't mean to *"abound again,"* it simply means "abundant" or "abounding"). Language is not static, but dynamic. Words change meaning over time. Today *"replenish"* means *"to fill again."* It didn't mean the same thing in 17th century England. Nearly all modern translations translate mâlê' as simply *"fill"* in the passage in question (Genesis 1:28).

Proponents of the Gap Theory respond by pointing out that God said to Noah after the flood, *"Be fruitful and multiply, and fill [mâlê'] the earth"* (Genesis 9:1). It is evident that Noah was meant to refill the earth after the flood. Can't we then interpret the same command to Adam to mean the same thing—that Adam was to repopulate the earth after God's judgment? The fact is that, regardless what the condition of the planet was before Noah's flood, God didn't tell Noah to "refill" the Earth. He simply said to fill it. God chose the words He chose and no others. If He said *"refill,"* that would have been something, but since He just said "fill," that argument falls flat.

The real problem with the Gap Theory is that it places human mortality (pre-Adamic human mortality) before Adam's sin. The Bible is quite clear that death entered in through Adam's sin. *"For since by a man came death, by a man also came the resurrection of the dead. For as in Adam all die, so also in Christ all will be made alive"* (1 Corinthians 15:21-22). Regardless of whether or not we believe in animal mortality before sin, the Bible is quite explicit about human mortality before Adam's sin. There wasn't any. To deny this is to deny a central Christian doctrine.

34. QUESTION:
"What is progressive creationism and is it biblical?"

ANSWER: Progressive creationism (also called *"process creation"*) is the belief that God created the heavens and the earth over a period of billions of years, not the six 24-hour days that is the basis for the traditional creationism view. Progressive creationists can be liberal or conservative in their theological belief system, but they generally agree on the following:

* The *"Big Bang"* was God's way of producing stars and galaxies through billions of years of natural processes.

* The earth and universe are billions of years old, not merely thousands of years old.

* The days of creation were overlapping periods of millions and billions of years.

* Death and bloodshed have existed from the very beginning of creation and were not the result of Adam's sin. Man was created after the vast majority of earth's history of life and death had already taken place.

* The flood of Noah was local, not global, and it had little effect on the earth's geology, which shows billions of years of history.

It is obvious that progressive creationism is a belief which opposes both atheistic evolutionism and historic Christianity's understanding of biblical creationism. The teachings of progressive creationism are not new or original, but, in recent years have received favorable publicity through Christian radio, television, magazines and books.

The error of progressive creationism rests on the assumption that the biblical account of creation in Genesis chapters 1-2 cannot be understood literally. According to progressive creationism, the *"days"* in Genesis chapter 1 are not literal 24-hour days, but actually long periods of time (millions or even billions of years). (See our article on the days of creation.) Progressive creationists accept the evolutionary viewpoint of the age of the earth, which is itself circularly based on evolution. It would take billions of years for evolution to have any chance of occurring; therefore, the earth must be billions of years old. (See our article on age of the earth.)

Another error of progressive creationism is that it posits that death existed prior to the Fall, which undermines the Bible's clear teaching that death is a result of sin (see Romans 5:12 and 1 Corinthians 15:21-22). Any theory which places the death of men or animals prior to the fall of Adam must be rejected.

Clearly, progressive creationism is an attempt by some Christians to harmonize the teachings of modern science with the Bible. However, the theory actually ends up supporting the tenets of evolutionary science and causes greater anxiety among believers about whether God's Word can be trusted. After all, the so-called *"proofs"* of progressive creationism come mainly from the field of science, not from the simple teachings of the Bible.

35. QUESTION:
"How does the geologic timescale fit with the view of a young earth?"

ANSWER: The question of how the geologic timescale fits with the *"young earth"* view is a good one. The earth's crust is made up of three different kinds of rock: igneous and metamorphic rock, both of which were once in a molten or semi-molten state, and sedimentary rock, rock which once existed elsewhere but was re-deposited as sediments in its current location. Sedimentary rock is usually layered. These layers are called *"strata."* Strata often contain the fossilized remains of plant and animal life which were buried and subsequently preserved through fossilization. Certain fossils have been found to be unique to certain layers. These fossils are called "index fossils." Paleontologists use index fossils to identify the rock layers in which they are found. If an index fossil is thought to be 70 million years old, then the rock layer in which it was found must also be 70 million years old. The *"geologic column"* is a sequential catalog of these layers, the fossils they contain, and the ages which have been assigned to the various geological eras which are thought to be represented in the geologic record.

Critics claim that the geologic column is flawed in that it relies upon circular reasoning. This is because the strata are not always found in the order in which they are supposed to be. Sometimes rock layers containing what are thought to be older fossils are found above rock layers which contain what are thought to be younger fossils (the younger fossils should be on top). Geologists reorganize the discrepant fossils and rock layers by using the assumed order in which the creatures were supposed to have evolved (this organism was supposed to have evolved before this one, so it goes here on bottom, while this organism was supposed to have evolved after this one so it goes here on top, etc.). Biologists then use the evolutionary progression organized by the geologists as evidence for evolutionary progression. This is a circular argument.

"A circular argument arises: Interpret the fossil record in the terms of a particular theory of evolution, inspect the interpretation, and note that it confirms the theory. Well, it would, wouldn't it?" (*"A Fresh Look at the Fossil Record,"* New Scientist, Vol. 108, December 1985, pg. 67) *"Are the authorities maintaining on the one hand, that evolution is documented by geology and, on the other hand, that geology is documented by evolution? Isn't this a circular argument?"* (Larry Azar, *"Biologists, Help!"* Bioscience, vol. 28, November 1978, p. 714).

We use the theory of evolution to interpret the fossil record. We then turn around and use our interpretations of the fossil record as evidence for the theory of evolution. *"And this poses something of a problem: If we date the rocks by the fossils, how can we then turn around and talk about the patterns of evolutionary change through time in the fossil record?"* (Niles Eldridge, Time Frames, 1985, p. 52) *"...Geologists are here arguing in a circle. The succession of organisms has been determined by a study of their remains embedded in the rocks, and the relative ages of the rocks are determined by the remains of organisms that they contain."* (R. H. Rastall, *"Geology,"* Encyclopedia Britannica, vol. 10, 1954, p. 168)

"The intelligent layman has long suspected circular reasoning in the use of rocks to date fossils and fossils to date rocks. The geologist has never bothered to think of a good reply, feeling that explanations are not worth the trouble as long as the work brings results. This is supposed to be hard-headed pragmatism." (J. E. O'Rourke, *"Pragmatism Versus Materialism in Stratigraphy,"* American Journal of Science, vol. 276, January 1976, p. 47)

The issue gets more complicated when we find discrepant fossils in the same rock layers! *"Frequently, fossils are not vertically sequenced in the assumed evolutionary order. For example, in Uzbekistan, 86 consecutive hoof prints of horses were found in rocks dating back to the dinosaurs. Hoof prints of some other animal are alongside 1,000 dinosaur footprints in Virginia.*

A leading authority on the Grand Canyon published photographs of horse-like hoof prints visible in rocks that, according to the theory of evolution, predate hoofed animals by more than 100 million years. Dinosaur and humanlike footprints were found together in Turkmenistan and Arizona. Sometimes, land animals, flying animals, and marine animals are fossilized side-by-side in the same rock. Dinosaur, whale, elephant, horse, and other fossils, plus crude human tools, have reportedly been found in phosphate beds in South Carolina. Coal beds contain round, black lumps called coal balls, some of which contain flowering plants that allegedly evolved 100 million years after the coal bed was formed. In the Grand Canyon, in Venezuela, in Kashmir, and in Guyana, spores of ferns and pollen from flowering plants are found in Cambrian rocks—rocks supposedly deposited before flowering plants evolved. Pollen has also been found in Precambrian rocks deposited before life allegedly evolved." (Walt Brown, In the Beginning, 7th edition., 2001, p. 11

"Petrified trees in Arizona's petrified forest contain fossilized nests of bees and cocoons of wasps. The petrified forests are reputedly 220 million years old, while bees (and flowering plants which bees require) supposedly evolved almost 100 million years later. Pollinating insects and fossil flies, with long, well-developed

tubes for sucking nectar from flowers, are dated 25 million years before flowers are assumed to have evolved. Most evolutionists and textbooks systematically ignore discoveries which conflict with the evolutionary time scale" (Brown, ibid).

Moreover, some of the index fossils which geologists use to date bygone eras have been found still alive today. Consider, for example, the coelacanth, an index fossil which was thought to have gone extinct 70 million years ago. *"...The coelacanth was a member of a very ancient class of fishes which was supposed to have disappeared some 70 million years ago. This great group of fishes, call crossopterygians, flourished during that decisive era in the history of the earth - when the fish, taking on legs and lungs, went forth to conquer the continents"* (Jacques Millot, *"The Coelacanths,"* Scientific American, vol. 193, December 1955, p. 37). It turns out the coelacanth didn't disappear *"some 70 million years ago."* They're still around today!

The first living coelacanth was caught in 1938 deep in the Indian Ocean, northwest of Madagascar. Since then, rewards have been offered for coelacanths, so hundreds have been caught and sold. Before 1938, evolutionists dated any rock containing a coelacanth fossil as at least 70 million years old. It was an index fossil. Today, evolutionists frequently express amazement that coelacanth fossils look so much like captured coelacanths - despite more than 70 million years of evolution. Before living coelacanths were caught, evolutionists incorrectly believed the coelacanth had lungs, a large brain, and four bottom fins about to evolve into legs. Evolutionists reasoned that the coelacanth, or a similar fish, must have crawled out of a shallow sea and filled its lungs with air, becoming the first four-legged land animal. Millions of students have been taught that this fish was the ancestor to all amphibians, reptiles, dinosaurs, birds, and mammals, including people. (Was your ancestor a fish?)

Professor J. L. B. Smith, a well-known fish expert from South Africa, who privately studied the first two captured coelacanths, nicknamed the coelacanth *"Old Fourlegs,"* and wrote a book by that title in 1956. However, in 1987, a German team led by Hans Fricke filmed six coelacanths in their natural habitat. *"Were they crawling on all fours in a shallow sea? Did they have lungs and a large brain? Not at all. In fact, they lived 500-1,200 feet below sea level and spent much of their time doing headstands, apparently looking for food"* (Walt Brown, In the Beginning, 2001, 7th edition, p. 29).

The point is that the geologic column may not be as reliable as many scientists and academics make it out to be. We urge everyone to investigate this matter for themselves before accepting any conclusions derived from this dubious dating method.

36. QUESTION:
"How does radiometric dating fit with the view of a young earth?"

ANSWER: Radiometric dating does not fit with the *"young earth"* view. Radiometric dating is a method which scientists use to determine the age of various specimens, mainly inorganic matter (rocks, etc.), though there is one radiometric dating technique, radiocarbon dating, which is used to date organic specimens.

How do these dating techniques work? Basically, scientists take advantage of a natural process by which unstable radioactive "parent" isotopes decay into stable *"daughter"* isotopes spontaneously over time. Uranium-238 (U238), for example, is an unstable radioactive isotope which decays into Lead-206 (Pb206) naturally over time (it goes through 13 unstable intermediate stages before it finally stabilizes into Pb206). In this case, U238 is the "parent" and Pb206 is the *"daughter."*

Scientists begin by measuring how long it takes for a parent isotope to decay into a daughter isotope. In this particular case, it takes 4,460,000,000 years for half of a sample of U238 to decay into Pb206. It takes another 4,460,000,000 years for half of the remaining sample to decay into Pb206 and then another 4,460,000,000 years for half of what's then left to decay, and so on. The time it takes for half of a sample to decay is called a *"half-life."*

By measuring radioactive half-lives, by measuring how much parent and daughter are present in any given specimen, and by making certain key assumptions, scientists believe they are able to accurately determine the age of a specimen. The measurements involved can be quite accurate. The question is what are the underlying key assumptions and how reliable are they?

The three key underlying assumptions are 1) the rate of

decay of parent into daughter has remained constant throughout the unobservable past; 2) the specimen which we are examining hasn't been contaminated in any way (that is, no parent or daughter has been added or taken away at any point during the unobservable past), and 3) we can determine how much parent and daughter were present at the beginning of the decay process – not all of the Pb206 present today necessarily came from decaying U238; Pb206 may have been part of the original constitution of the specimen. If any of these assumptions are wrong, the metho cannot accurately determine the age of a specimen.

While the second and third assumptions have always been a bit troublesome, especially the third assumption, which considers the original constitution of a particular specimen, the first assumption was thought to be a pretty safe bet since scientists were not able to vary the decay rates much in a lab. Recently, however, new research has revealed that the decay rates may have been drastically different in the unobservable past. This calls the whole method into question. AiG's Dr. Carl Wieland explains, *"When uranium decays to lead, a by-product of this process is the formation of helium, a very light, inert gas which readily escapes from rock. Certain crystals called zircons, obtained from drilling into very deep granites, contain uranium which has partly decayed into lead. By measuring the amount of uranium and 'radiogenic lead' in these crystals, one can calculate that, if the decay rate has been constant, about 1.5 billion years must have passed. (This is consistent with the geologic 'age' assigned to the granites in which these zircons are found.) There is a significant amount of helium from that '1.5 billion years of decay' still inside the zircons. This is at first glance surprising for long-agers, because of the ease with which one would expect helium (with its tiny, light, unreactive atoms) to escape from the spaces within the crystal structure. There should surely be hardly any left, because with such a slow buildup, it should be seeping out continually and not accumulating. …Results show that because of all the helium still in the zircons, these crystals (and since this is Precambrian basement granite, by implication the whole earth) could not be older than between 4,000 and 14,000 years. In other words, in only a few thousand years, 1.5 billion years' worth (at today's rates) of radioactive decay has taken place"*

37. QUESTION:
"Is there any evidence for the Bible's view of a young earth?"

ANSWER: There is a profusion of evidence for the Bible's view of a young earth. However, the old-earth perspective has held a monopoly in the public schools, in the major academic centers, and in the popular media for generations. It is no wonder then that most scientists share the old-earth perspective. It's all they were taught growing up in school. It's all they learned at the universities where they got their degrees. It's what most of their colleagues profess. But there are dissenters among the scientific community, and their numbers are growing. Why? Because more and more scientists are confronting a growing body of evidence which challenges the old-earth paradigm.

This is not to say that everyone who examines these evidences will reject the old-earth perspective. Some who have pondered these evidences regard them as anomalous, yet-to-be-explained phenomena. Some believe they don't stand up under close scrutiny. Some view them as deliberate misrepresentations of the facts by religious zealots.

There is no doubt that religious zealots have a tendency to distort facts when it suits their purposes. old-earth zealots have the same tendency when their careers and reputations are on the line. It's human nature. It is also true that some of the young-earth evidences which have been proposed over the years have not withstood close scrutiny. But many others have, and the fact remains that a growing number of professionally trained scientists—experts in their fields—are accepting a young-earth perspective as being at least scientifically plausible, if not compelling. Here are a few of the relevant evidences for consideration:

CONTINENTAL EROSION AND FOSSIL REMAINS. The continents are eroding at such a rate that, if not for tectonic uplift, meteoric dusting and volcanic influx, they would erode flat (Mt. Everest and all) in less than 25 million years. At this rate, high-altitude, million-year-old fossils should have long since eroded away. And yet they remain. The implication is that these fossils are not millions of years old. If this were true, the entire geologic column would need serious revision.

SUBTERRANEAN FLUID PRESSURE. When a drill rig strikes oil, the oil sometimes gushes out in huge fountains.

This is because the oil is often under huge amounts of pressure from the sheer weight of the rock sitting on top of it. Other subterranean fluids kept under pressure include natural gas and water. The problem is, the rock above many pressurized subterranean fluid deposits is relatively permeable. The pressure should escape in less than 100,000 years. Yet these deposits remain highly pressurized. Once again, because of the supposed antiquity of these deposits and their location throughout the geologic column, this observation calls into question some of the interpretations which have led to the formulation of the column.

GLOBAL COOLING. In the 19th century, the renowned physicist and inventor Lord Kelvin (William Thomson) was the first to point out that if the earth began in a white-hot molten state, it would have cooled to its current temperature billions of years sooner than the 4.6 billion years accepted today. Since then, old-earth advocates have pointed out that radioactive decay within the earth would greatly slow down the cooling process. Young-earth advocates respond that, even given liberal assumptions concerning the amount of heat produced by radioactive decay, the earth would still cool to its current temperature much sooner than old earth advocates allow.

Lunar Recession. The moon is slowly moving farther away from the earth. This has to do with the fact that the earth's spin is slowing down due to tidal friction and other factors. Lunar recession was first observed by Edmund Halley in the late 1600s (the same Edmund Halley who is credited with being the first to predict the 76-year orbit of the famous comet which bears his name). Given the rate of lunar recession today, the fact that it has gradually accelerated over time, and several other factors, physicists have determined that the earth-moon system could not have existed beyond 1.2 billion years. (This is 3.4 billion years less time than old-earth advocates are willing to accept. Furthermore, the closer the moon gets to the earth, the greater its influence on our tides. We can't go too far back in time before we would all drown twice a day.

Helium diffusion from Precambrian Zircons. Helium is produced within the earth by the radioactive decay of certain unstable elements (uranium and thorium being two such elements). Some of this decay takes place inside of crystals known as *"zircons."* Helium diffuses from these zircons at known rates depending upon depth and temperature. Scientists have discovered that, in zircons where a billion years of uranium decay has allegedly taken place, too much helium remains—way too much helium. It appears as if the helium hasn't had enough time to diffuse out of the crystals. This observation has a couple of implications.

First, this observation may overturn a key assumption underlying radiometric dating (the most common old-earth dating technique). Scientists believe that a billion years of uranium decay has taken place within these zircons because they make certain assumptions about the unobservable past. One of these assumptions is that radioactive decay has remained constant throughout the unobservable past. Scientists have been able to vary decay rates in the lab, but most don't believe that it actually happens in nature. However, if billions years of uranium decay has taken place so quickly that the helium produced hasn't had enough time to escape the zircons, this may be strong evidence that radioactive decay rates were greatly accelerated in the unobservable past.

Second, because the zircons came from Precambrian rocks below the geologic column, currently accepted old-earth interpretations of the geologic column may need serious revision. These and numerous other scientific evidences for a young-earth theory give credence to the Bible's account of the creation of the earth and universe as found in Genesis.

38. QUESTION:
"Is the theory of Pangea possible? Does the Bible say that there was once a Pangea / Pangaea?"

ANSWER: Pangea is the concept that all of the land masses of the earth were at one time connected as one giant super-continent. On a world map, some of the continents look like they could fit together like giant puzzle pieces (Africa and South America, for example). Does the Bible mention Pangea? Not explicitly, but possibly. Genesis 1:9 records, *"And God said, 'Let the water under the sky be gathered to one place, and let dry ground appear.' And it was so."* Presumably, if all the water was *"gathered to one place,"* the dry ground would also be all *"in one place."* Genesis 10:25 mentions, *"...one was named Peleg, because in his time the earth was divided..."* Some point to Genesis 10:25 as evidence that the earth was divided after the Flood of Noah.

While this view is possible, it is most definitely not

universally held by Christians. Some view Genesis 10:25 as referring to the *"division"* that occurred at the Tower of Babel, not the division of the continents via *"continental drift."* Some also dispute the post-Noahic Pangea separation due to the fact that, at the current rates of drift, the continents could not possibly have drifted so far apart in the time that has transpired since the Noahic Flood. However, it cannot be proven that the continents have always drifted at the same rate. Further, God is capable of expediting the continental-drift process to accomplish His goal of separating humanity (Genesis 11:8). Again, though, the Bible does not explicitly mention Pangea, or conclusively tell us when Pangea was broken apart.

The post-Noahic Pangea concept does possibly explain how the animals and humanity were able to migrate to the different continents. How did the kangaroos get to Australia after the Flood if the continents were already separated? Young-earth creationist alternatives to the standard continental drift theory include the Catastrophist Plate Tectonics Theory , both of which place accelerated continental drift within the cataclysmic context of Noah's Flood.

However, there is another explanation offered by Christian scientists that does not require a post-Noahic Pangea. According to this view, intercontinental migration most likely began while sea levels were still low during and immediately following the post-Flood Ice Age when much of the water was still trapped in ice at the poles. Lower sea levels would have left the continental shelves exposed, connecting all of the major land masses through land bridges.

There are (or at least were) shallow underwater land bridges connecting all of the major continents. North America, Southeast Asia, and Australia are all attached to continental Asia. Britain is attached to continental Europe. In some places, these intercontinental bridges are only a few hundred feet below our current sea level. The theory can be summarized as follows: (1) After the Flood, an Ice Age occurred. (2) The vast amount of water that was frozen resulted in the oceans being much lower than they are today. (3) The low level of the oceans resulted in land bridges connecting the various continents. (4) Human beings and animals migrated to the different continents over these land bridges. (5) The Ice Age ended, the ice melted and the ocean levels rose, resulting in the land bridges being submerged.

So, while Pangea is not explicitly mentioned in the Bible, the Bible does present the possibility of a Pangea. Whatever the case, either view presented above presents a viable explanation for how humanity and animals were able to migrate to continents now separated by vast oceans.

39. Question:
"What is the Anthropic Principle?"

Answer: Anthropic means *"relating to human beings or their existence."* Principle means *"law."* The Anthropic Principle is the Law of Human Existence. It is well known that our existence in this universe depends on numerous cosmological constants and parameters whose numerical values must fall within a very narrow range of values. If even a single variable were off, even slightly, we would not exist. The extreme improbability that so many variables would align so auspiciously in our favor merely by chance has led some scientists and philosophers to propose instead that it was God who providentially engineered the universe to suit our specific needs. This is the Anthropic Principle: that the universe appears to have been fine-tuned for our existence.

Consider protons, for example. Protons are the positively charged subatomic particles which (along with neutrons) form the nucleus of an atom (around which negatively charged electrons orbit). Whether by providence or fortuitous luck (depending on your perspective), protons just happen to be 1,836 times larger than electrons. If they were a little bigger or a little smaller, we would not exist (because atoms could not form the molecules we require). So how did protons end up being 1,836 times larger than electrons? Why not 100 times larger or 100,000 times? Why not smaller? Of all the possible variables, how did protons end up being just the right size? Was it luck or contrivance?

Or how is it that protons carry a positive electrical charge equal to that of the negatively charged electrons? If protons did not balance electrons and vice versa, we would not exist. They are not comparable in size, yet they are perfectly balanced. Did nature just stumble upon such a propitious relationship, or did God ordain it for our sakes?

Here are some examples of how the Anthropic Principle directly affects the livability of our planet:

THE UNIQUE PROPERTIES OF WATER. Every known life form depends on water. Thankfully, unlike every other substance known to man, water's solid form (ice) is less dense than its liquid form. This causes ice to float. If ice did not float, our planet would experience runaway freezing. Other important properties of water include its solvency, cohesiveness, adhesiveness and other thermal properties.

EARTH'S ATMOSPHERE. If there were too much of just one of the many gases which make up our atmosphere, our planet would suffer a runaway greenhouse effect. On the other hand, if there were not enough of these gases, life on this planet would be devastated by cosmic radiation.

EARTH'S REFLECTIVITY OR "ALBEDO" (the total amount of light reflected off the planet versus the total amount of light absorbed). If Earth's albedo were much greater than it is now, we would experience runaway freezing. If it were much less than it is, we would experience a runaway greenhouse effect.

EARTH'S MAGNETIC FIELD. If it were much weaker, our planet would be devastated by cosmic radiation. If it were much stronger, we would be devastated by severe electromagnetic storms.

EARTH'S PLACE IN THE SOLAR SYSTEM. If we were much further from the sun, our planet's water would freeze. If we were much closer, it would boil. This is just one of numerous examples of how our privileged place in the solar system allows for life on Earth.

OUR SOLAR SYSTEM'S PLACE IN THE GALAXY. Once again, there are numerous examples of this. For instance, if our solar system were too close to the center of our galaxy, or to any of the spiral arms at its edge, or any cluster of stars, for that matter, our planet would be devastated by cosmic radiation.

THE COLOR OF OUR SUN. If the sun were much redder, on the one hand, or bluer, on the other, photosynthesis would be impeded. Photosynthesis is a natural biochemical process crucial to life on Earth.

The above list is by no means exhaustive. It is just a small sample of the many factors which must be just right in order for life to exist on Earth. We are very fortunate to live on a privileged planet in a privileged solar system in a privileged galaxy in a privileged universe.

The question for us now is, with so many universal constants and cosmological parameters defining our universe, and with so many possible variables for each one, how did they all just happen to fall within the extremely narrow range of values required for our existence? The general consensus is that we are either here by fortuitous luck against tremendous odds or by the purposeful design of an intelligent Agent.

Some proponents of the here-by-chance perspective have sought to level the odds against fortuitous luck by hypothesizing a scenario whereby our universe is just one among many in what has come to be termed a "multiverse." This gives nature many more chances to "get it right," bringing the odds against its success down significantly.

Imagine innumerable lifeless universes in which one or more of the necessary variables fail to fall within the specific range of values required for life. The idea is that nature would eventually get it right, and apparently has done so as evidenced by the fact that we exist (or so the argument goes). We are the lucky ones whose universe stumbled upon the right combination of cosmological values. The Anthropic Principle is often cited as empirical grounds for the otherwise mathematically hypothetical multiverse.

Intelligent Design theorists hail the Anthropic Principle as further evidence in support of their thesis that life was engineered by a transcendent Mastermind. Not only do biological systems bear the hallmarks of design (the information content of DNA, specified complexity, irreducible complexity, etc.), but the universe which supports and provides a context for life appears to have been designed as a means to that end.

40. QUESTION:
"Did the Bible copy some of its stories from other religious myths and legends?"

ANSWER: There are many stories in the Bible that have remarkable similarities with stories from other religions, legends, and myths. For the purposes of this article, we will examine two of the more prominent examples. For a detailed comparison of Noah's Flood and the Gilgamesh Epic, see - Did the Bible copy the Flood account from other myths and legends?

First, let's consider the account of the Fall of mankind from

Genesis chapter 3. There is a Greek legend, that of Pandora's Box, whose details differ so dramatically from the biblical account of the Fall that one might never suspect a relationship. But despite their significant differences, they may actually attest to the same historical event. Both stories tell how the very first woman unleashed sin, sickness, and suffering upon the world which had been, up to that point, an Edenic paradise. Both stories end with the emergence of hope, hope in a promised Redeemer in the case of Genesis, and "hope" as a thing having been released from the box at the very end of the Pandora legend.

Like the world's copious flood legends, Pandora's Box demonstrates how the Bible might parallel pagan myths at times simply because they all speak of an historical core truth which has over the years manifested itself in ancient histories (as in the case of the Bible) and in poetic allegories (as in the case of Pandora, whose story was told in many different ways by the Greeks but whose core truth remained fairly constant). The similarities do not point to one account copying from the other, but rather, to the fact that both stories point back to the same historical event.

Finally, there are cases of borrowing, but in these cases the

Bible was the source, not the pagan myths (despite pseudo-academic claims to the contrary). Consider the case of Sargon's birth. Legend has it that Sargon was placed in a reed basket and sent down the river by his mother. He was rescued by Aqqi, who then adopted him as his own son. Sounds a lot like the story Moses in Exodus 2, doesn't it? And Sargon lived about 800 years before Moses was born. So the Moses baby-sent-down-the-river-only-to-be-rescued-and-adopted story must have been borrowed from Sargon, right?

That sounds reasonable on the face of it, but what is known of Sargon comes almost entirely from legends written many hundreds of years after his death. There are very few contemporary records of Sargon's life. The legend of Sargon's childhood, how he was placed in a basket and sent down a river, comes from two 7th century BC cuneiform tablets (from the library of the Assyrian king Ashurbanipal, who reigned from 668 to 627 BC), written hundreds of years after the book of Exodus. If someone wants to argue that one account was borrowed from another, it would have to be the other way around: the Sargon legend appears to have borrowed from the Exodus account of Moses.

The Bible is clear as to its authorship. Although many

different men put pen to paper, the Holy Spirit of God is the actual author. Second Timothy 3:16-17 tells us that Scripture is inspired by God.

41. QUESTION:
"What is the Serpent Seed doctrine?"

ANSWER: The serpent seed doctrine is a belief based on poor biblical interpretation and superstition. It is a primary doctrinal resource for those who want to use Scriptures to justify racial prejudice. The serpent seed doctrine is also closely related to other erroneous beliefs such as the Christian Identity Movement and the Kenite doctrine. Like many false beliefs, it has a built-in defense mechanism; that is, anyone who disagrees with it is accused of being a son of the serpent. One of the most unfortunate problems with the serpent seed doctrine is that is so heavily relies on prejudice and warped biblical interpretation that it can be very difficult to discuss rationally.

Simply stated, the serpent seed doctrine teaches that the sin of Eve was not simple disobedience, but sexual contact with the serpent, and that Cain was the son of Eve and the devil. Cain's descendants are, according to this idea, the sons of Satan, and this includes most any race or group that the serpent-seed believer chooses to dislike. This idea is rooted in superstitious beliefs and is particularly popular with white supremacists and anti-Semites; the Unification Church also supports this idea. Noted false prophets and false teachers such as Arnold Murray of Shepherd's Chapel and William Branham espoused the idea. Although an idea should not be criticized when it is wrongly applied, it is appropriate to condemn an idea when it logically leads to sin. A philosophy that teaches that some races or people are universally satanic, like the serpent seed doctrine, is one such philosophy.

Those who support serpent-seed ideas cite many passages in the Bible as proof that their idea is correct. Almost without exception, these *"proofs"* require an interpretation that is totally inappropriate to the context of the passage. For example, Genesis 3:13 is often cited, with the claim that the word translated *"beguiled"* in the King James Version really meant *"seduced."* Context and scholarship would disagree. Proverbs 30:20 metaphorically compares eating and sexual immorality; this is greatly overstated by the serpent-seed believer as proof that the Fall was sexual. Other passages include Jude 1:14, and the parable of the tares in Matthew chapter 13. Those who believe in the serpent seed doctrine teach that Jesus' description of the *"children of the devil"* in this parable is true in a biological sense. Again, only one who is trying to force this belief into the Bible will see it this way; it is not naturally read out of Scripture.

There are literally dozens of places in the Bible where this false idea has been wedged in, yet every single one requires a person to believe in the serpent-seed idea beforehand. Only by reading a passage and saying, *"If you assume that the serpent seed doctrine is true, then this means…"* can a person support this false philosophy. For this reason, arguing against the serpent seed doctrine can be difficult. Those who believe it interpret Scripture through a sort of *"serpent-seed lens,"* and are not likely to accept other interpretations, no matter how well supported by context and scholarship.

There are some basic questions and contradictions inherent to the serpent seed doctrine that can be used to demonstrate its lack of truth. For example, Galatians 3:28 clearly states that race and gender have no impact on our standing with God. Second Peter 3:9 says that God wants everyone to be saved, not *"everyone but the children of Cain."* Nowhere in Scripture is anyone identified as a *"Kenite"* or condemned based on being from Cain's lineage. Never are we warned about such people by the New Testament writers. Also, there is the question of how or why such persons survived the flood. The doctrine supposes that original sin was sexual, but cannot explain why the whole remainder of the Bible lays out a worldview where the original sin was disobedience, not sexuality.

This philosophy is most unfortunate in that it leads directly and logically to two main problems. Racism is by far the worst; believing that certain races are irredeemable has no positive application. The only possible outcome of such a worldview is prejudice and bigotry. There is also a tendency to dismiss critics of the serpent seed doctrine as being the very *"Kenites"* the philosophy believes in. Arnold Murray is particularly guilty of this abuse. Fortunately for believers, God has given us a resource in Scripture that can show us the truth. We need only read it with unbiased and open eyes to find true wisdom.

42. QUESTION:
"What is the Table of Nations?"

ANSWER: Genesis chapter 10, commonly known as the Table of Nations, is a list of the patriarchal founders of seventy nations which descended from Noah through his three sons, Shem, Ham and Japheth. Twenty-six of the seventy descended from Shem, thirty from Ham and fourteen from Japheth. The 32nd verse sums up the chapter succinctly: "These are the families of the sons of Noah, according to their genealogies, by their nations; and out of these the nations were separated on the earth after the flood." Chapter 11 recounts their division at Babel.

The text seems to imply, though it never explicitly states, that the list was intended to be an exhaustive account. It has traditionally been interpreted as such. Nevertheless, this interpretation is speculative.

All of the Biblical genealogies are abridged. Key historical figures are included while *"lesser,"* or less culturally relevant, siblings are left out. It is possible that such is the case for the Table of Nations. The compiler of the Table may have focused his ethnology on the nations most significant to his own nation at the time of the Table's compilation, while neglecting the founders of other far-flung, perhaps even long-forgotten nations. While every nation is ultimately related to every other nation through Noah, this ancestral tie does not indefinitely perpetuate mutual cultural significance among his descendants. As the old adage goes, *"Out of sight, out of mind."*

While some of the nations listed are easily identifiable, some remain obscure. Numerous scholars have attempted to identify these unknown nations with varying degrees of success. Due to the archaic nature of the source material, there remains considerable ambiguity.

The accuracy of the Table has been called into question by the fact that some of the relationships described do not match up with modern comparative linguistics. For example, the Elamites are said to have descended from Shem, yet their language was not Semitic. The Canaanites are said to have descended from Ham, yet their language was Semitic.

This objection assumes that these languages never experienced any dramatic change. The region's history seems to suggest that this is a dubious assumption. The cultures of the region were constantly subject to migrations and invasions by foreign powers. The conquering empires often imposed their language and culture upon the vanquished.

The Hellenizing of the Persian Empire following Alexander the Great's conquest is a classic example. Or consider the Israelites, who primarily spoke ancient Hebrew up until the Babylonian captivity and the Persian conquest. Then they adopted Aramaic, the official language of the Persian Empire. The Jewish Talmud was written in Aramaic, as were large portions of the books of Daniel and Ezra. Aramaic is thought to have been Jesus' native language. Following Alexander's conquest of Persia, the Jews adopted Greek as a second language. As a result, all of the New Testament was written in Greek. The languages of the region were not static.

The Hebrews invaded and conquered Canaan long before the Greeks, Persians and Babylonians. Is it any wonder that the Canaanites of the region adopted a Semitic language almost identical to ancient Hebrew? As for the Elamites, if we want to make a case from Elamite we have to start with proto-Elamite. Proto-Elamite remains undeciphered, so it cannot form the basis for a polemic against the Table of Nations. There is no evidence that the later, non-Semitic Elamite underlies proto-Elamite, and we do not know what influences may have altered the language at any time.

Another objection to the Table of Nations is that several of the nations listed do not appear in the historical record (as we have it today) until as late as the first millennium B.C. This has led some critical scholars to date the Table no earlier than 7th century B.C.

This is a recurring criticism of the Bible. Rather than give the Bible the benefit of the doubt whenever it mentions a city or culture that doesn't appear anywhere else in the historical record, or whenever it places a culture in an era that antedates any other record we have from our other limited sources, critics generally assume that the biblical authors were either disingenuous or ignorant. Such was the case for the ancient metropolis of Nineveh and the ancient Hittite civilization of the Levant, both of which were rediscovered in modern times, in the 19th and 20th centuries, respectively, in a remarkable vindication of the Bible's historical witness. The fact of the matter is our knowledge of ancient cultures is extremely fragmented and often dependent upon key assumptions. It is therefore speculative to argue that the Table of Nations was written so late based solely on the fact that some of the nations mentioned appear nowhere else than in later historical records.

One final objection concerns the fact that Nimrod is said to have been a son of Cush (10:8), who is believed to have founded Nubia just south of Egypt. Yet Nimrod established several cities in Mesopotamia that show no sign of Nubian origin (10:8-12). Does this mean, as some critics claim, that the Table is therefore manifestly wrong, either about Nimrod's lineage or his role in establishing the Mesopotamian cities?

Skeptics who make this argument overlook the fact that Cush also fathered the founders of at least six Arabian nations (10:7), none of which show signs of Nubian origin. This is because Nubia developed along its own cultural path over many generations. Nimrod was an immediate son of Cush. We have no reason to expect him or the cities he helped establish to show any sign of Nubian origin.

In summary, the Table of Nations presents the biblical, ethnological view that all nations descend from Noah through three of his sons, Shem, Ham and Japheth. It is not known whether the list of seventy was meant to be exhaustive or if there were some nations left out, intentionally or accidentally. The accuracy of what we do know about the Table has been called into question by skeptics whose polemical objections tend to be defective and insubstantial. Due to the archaic nature of the source material, the veracity of the Table ultimately remains undeterminable. In the end, those who accept it do so by faith, taking it for granted as part of a larger, justifiable perspective. Those who reject it essentially do so for the same reasons.

43. QUESTION:
"Is creationism scientific?"

ANSWER: There is currently a lot of debate over the validity of creationism, defined as *"the belief that the universe and living organisms originate from specific acts of divine creation, as in the biblical account, rather than by natural processes such as evolution."* Creation science is often dismissed by the secular community and accused of lacking scientific value. However, creationism is clearly compatible with a scientific approach to any topic. Creationism makes statements about real world events, places, and things. It is not concerned solely with subjective ideas or abstract concepts. There are established scientific facts that are consistent with creationism, and the way in which those facts relate to one another lends itself to a creationist interpretation. Just as other broad scientific ideas are used to lend coherence to a series of facts, so, too, does creationism.

How, then, is creationism—as opposed to *"naturalism,"* defined as *"a philosophical viewpoint according to which everything arises from natural properties and causes, and supernatural or spiritual explanations are excluded or discounted"*—scientific? Admittedly, the answer depends on how you define *"scientific."* Too often, *"science"* and *"naturalism"* are considered one and the same, leaving creationist views out by definition. Such a definition requires an irrational reverence of naturalism. Science is defined as *"the observation, identification, description, experimental investigation, and theoretical explanation of phenomena."* Nothing requires science, in and of itself, to be naturalistic. Naturalism, like creationism, requires a series of presuppositions that are not generated by experiments. They are not extrapolated from data or derived from test results.

These philosophical presuppositions are accepted before any data is ever taken. Because both naturalism and creationism are strongly influenced by presuppositions that are neither provable nor testable, and enter into the discussion well before the facts do, it is fair to say that creationism is at least as scientific as naturalism.

Creationism, like naturalism, can be *"scientific,"* in that it is compatible with the scientific method of discovery. These two concepts are not, however, sciences in and of themselves, because both views include aspects that are not considered "scientific" in the normal sense. Neither creationism nor naturalism is falsifiable; that is, there is no experiment that could conclusively disprove either one. Neither one is predictive; they do not generate or enhance the ability to predict an outcome. Solely on the basis of these two points, we see that there is no logical reason to consider one more scientifically valid than the other.

One of the major reasons naturalists give for rejecting creationism is the concept of miracles. Ironically, naturalists will typically say that miracles, such as special creation, are impossible because they violate the laws of nature, which have been clearly and historically observed. Such a view is ironic on several counts. As a single example, consider abiogenesis, the theory of life springing from non-living matter. Abiogenesis is one of the most thoroughly refuted concepts of science. Yet, a truly naturalistic viewpoint presumes that life on earth—self-replicating, self-sustaining, complex organic life—arose by chance from non-living matter. Such a thing has never been observed in all of human history. The beneficial evolutionary changes needed to progress a creature to a more complex form have also never been observed. So creationism actually holds the edge on evidence for *"miraculous"* claims in that the Scriptures provide documented accounts of miraculous happenings. To label creationism as unscientific on account of miracles demands a similar label for naturalism.

There are many facts that are used by both sides of the creation vs. naturalism debate. Facts are facts, but there is no such thing as a fact that absolutely requires a single interpretation. The divide between creationism and secular naturalism rests entirely on different interpretations. Regarding the evolution vs. creation debate specifically, Charles Darwin himself made this point. In the introduction to The Origin of Species, he stated, *"I am well aware that scarcely a single point is discussed in this volume on which facts cannot be adduced, often apparently leading to conclusions directly opposite to those at which I arrived."* Obviously, Darwin believed evolution over creation, but he was willing to admit that interpretation was key to choosing a belief. One scientist might view a particular fact as supportive of naturalism; another scientist might view that same fact as supporting creationism.

Also, the fact that creationism is the only possible alternative to naturalistic ideas such as evolution makes it a valid topic, especially when this dichotomy has been admitted to by some of the leading minds of science. Many well-known and influential scientists state that the only possible explanations for life are naturalistic evolution or special creation. Not all scientists agree on which is true, but they almost all agree that one or the other must be.

There are many other reasons why creationism is a rational and scientific approach to learning. Among these are the concepts of realistic probability, the flawed evidential support for macro-evolution, the evidence of experience, and so forth. There is no logical basis to accept naturalistic presuppositions outright and flatly reject creationist presuppositions. Firm belief in creation is no barrier to scientific discovery. Simply review the accomplishments of men like Newton, Pasteur, Mendel, Pascal, Kelvin, Linnaeus, and Maxwell. All were clear and comfortable creationists. Creationism is not a *"science,"* just as naturalism is not a *"science."* Creationism is, however, fully compatible with science itself.

44. QUESTION:
"How does creationism vs. evolution impact how a person views the world?"

ANSWER: The key difference between creationism and evolution comes down to our certainty about everything we think we know. Think about it: if our five senses and our brains are merely the product of random, purposeless evolution, how can we be sure that they're giving us reliable information? The thing that my eye and brain perceives as *"red"* might be perceived by your eye and brain as *"blue,"* but you call it *"red"* because that's what you've been taught. (The colors themselves won't actually change, since they consist of certain, unchangeable frequencies of the electromagnetic spectrum.) We have no sure way of knowing we're talking about the same thing.

Or suppose you see a rock that seemed to have carving on it that reads *"Chicago: 50 miles."* Now also suppose you believe that those markings really are nothing but the result of random erosion from wind and rain that just appear to spell out this message. Could you have any real confidence that Chicago is really 50 miles away?

But what if you knew that every normal set of eyes and brains is designed to perceive a certain frequency of the electromagnetic spectrum as *"red"*? Then you can have confidence in knowing that what I see as red is also what you see as red. And what if you knew that a man had carefully measured the distance 50 miles from Chicago and then put a marker there to indicate that? Then you can have confidence that that marker is giving you accurate information.

Another difference in how creationism vs. evolution affects a person's view of the world is in the realm of morality. If we are merely the products of random, purposeless evolution, what, precisely, do the terms *"good"* and *"evil"* mean? *"Good"* as compared to what? *"Evil"* as compared to what? Indeed, without a measuring stick (e.g., God's nature), we have no basis for saying that something is good or evil; it is merely an opinion, which really has no weight in judging how I act or how I judge the acts of others. Mother Teresa and Stalin simply made different choices in such a world. There is no answer to the ultimate *"Says who?"* when it comes to determining right and wrong. And while atheists and evolutionists can certainly lead moral lives—if they were true to their beliefs they would have no reason to—nor would they have any basis to judge the actions of those they determine to have done something *"wrong."*

But if there is a God who created us in His image, then we are not only created with a sense of what is right or wrong, but we also have an answer to *"Says who?"* Good is what comports with God's nature, and evil is anything that does not.

45. QUESTION:
"Why is the science community so opposed to creationism?"

ANSWER: It is important to distinguish between the terms *"science"* and *"scientific community."* Science is a discipline concerned with observing, experimenting with, and explaining phenomena. The scientific community is composed of the living human persons who participate in this discipline. The distinction is important, because there is no logical contradiction between science and creationism. Science is a generic term for a type of study, while creationism is a philosophy applied to the interpretation of facts. The scientific community, as it exists today, holds naturalism as the preferred philosophy, but there is no overt reason why naturalism should be preferred by science over creationism.

In general, there is a perception that creationism is *"unscientific."* This is partly true, in the sense that creationism entails certain assumptions that cannot be tested, proven, or falsified. However, naturalism is in exactly the same predicament, as an untestable, unprovable, non-falsifiable philosophy. The facts discovered in scientific research are only that: facts. Facts and interpretations are two different things. The current scientific community rejects, in general, the concepts of creationism, and so they define it as *"unscientific."* This is highly ironic, given the scientific community's preference for an interpretive philosophy—naturalism—that is just as *"unscientific"* as creationism.

There are many reasons for this tendency towards naturalism in science. Creationism involves the intervention of a supernatural being, and science is primarily concerned with tangible and physical things. For this reason, some in the scientific community fear that creationism will lead to a *"God of the Gaps"* dilemma, where scientific questions are shrugged off by the explanation, *"God did it."* Experience has shown that this is not the case. Some of the greatest names in scientific history were staunch creationists. Their belief in God inspired them to ask, *"How did God do it?"* Among these names are Pascal, Maxwell, and Kelvin. On the other hand, an unreasonable commitment to naturalism can degrade scientific discovery. A naturalistic framework requires a scientist to ignore results that do not fit the established paradigm. That is, when new data does not correlate to the naturalistic view, it is assumed to be invalid and discarded.

There are distinct religious overtones to creationism. Science is only as objective as those who participate in it, and those persons are just as subject to bias as in any other field. There are those who reject creationism in favor of naturalism purely for personal *"moral"* reasons. In fact, this number is probably much higher than would be admitted to. Most people who reject the concepts of God do so primarily because they disagree with some perceived restriction or unfairness, despite claims to the contrary, and this is as true for those in lab coats as those in coveralls.

In the same way, an unfriendly attitude in the scientific community has had its impact on the perception of creationism. Science has benefited from creationist contributors for centuries; yet today the scientific community, at large, takes a hostile and condescending attitude towards anyone who doesn't take a naturalistic perspective. This open hostility towards creationist views, and religion in general, creates a strong incentive for persons with those views to avoid scientific study. Those who do often feel compelled to remain silent for fear of ridicule. In this way, the scientific community has degraded and *"pushed out"* a segment of the population, and then has the audacity to claim that a lowered percentage of creationists in their ranks is evidence of naturalism's superior scientific merit.

There are also political reasons for the scientific community's hostility towards creationism and religion in general. Christianity, more so than any other religious system, places immense value on every individual human life. This causes tensions with the scientific community when that concern for life gets in the way of some type of scientific process. Christian values tend to act as a brake on experiments or positions that cause harm to people, or that destroy or damage human life. Examples include embryonic stem cell research, abortion, and euthanasia. In other cases, Christian values butt heads with secular ones when science promotes certain sinful activities by making them easier. While naturalistic scientists may see this as an unnecessary hindrance, they should consider what happens when scientific research is conducted with no regard for morality or conscience. Echoing this idea was actor Jeff Goldblum's character in the movie Jurassic Park. He stated, *"Your scientists were so preoccupied with whether or not they could, they didn't stop to think if they should."*

There is also a level of competition between the scientific community and the religious community over power, producing additional tensions between science and creationism. As even some leading skeptic scientists have admitted, there is a tendency for the scientific community to position itself, even subconsciously, as a priesthood. This secular priesthood has the wondrous and elite knowledge that the laymen need for salvation, and cannot be questioned by any outsiders. In plain terms, religiously tinged ideas, such as creationism, impinge on the scientific community's claim to superior knowledge of the universe.

While there may be many reasons for tension between the scientific community and creationism, there are plenty of reasons why they should be able to coexist peacefully. There are no logically valid reasons to reject creationism in favor of naturalism, as the scientific community has done. Creationism does not inhibit discovery, as evidenced by the titans of science who believed strongly in it. The derisive attitude spewed at creationists has diminished the number of capable and willing minds in many fields. Creationism has much to offer science and the scientific community. The God who made the universe revealed Himself through it (Psalm 19:1); the more we know about His creation, the more glory He receives!

46. QUESTION:
"What caused the extinction of the dinosaurs?"

ANSWER: The extinction of the dinosaurs is an enigma that has captivated scientists for well over a century. We find the fossilized remains of giant reptiles all over the earth, yet we do not see any of these creatures alive today. What happened to them all?

The conventional paradigm says that they mysteriously disappeared around 65 million years ago. An assortment of explanations has been offered as to why. The two most popular hypotheses are the Impact Event Hypothesis and the Massive Volcanism Hypothesis. The first proposes that one or more asteroids struck the earth, causing a *"nuclear winter"* which wiped out the dinosaurs. The second blames intense volcanism for their demise. Both make note of the high concentration of Iridium (Ir) found buried in the sediments which separate the Cretaceous period from the Paleogene (known as the K-Pg boundary; formerly known as the K-T boundary), which, according to the conventional paradigm, was the period in Earth's history during which the dinosaurs went extinct.

Both hypotheses take some of the evidence into account while ignoring some. For example, if either hypothesis is correct and there is a 60+ million-year gap between man and dinosaur, how then do we explain petroglyphs and other forms of ancient art which depict humans interacting with such familiar dinosaurs as the triceratops, stegosaurus, tyrannosaurus and the sauropods (in some cases taming them and riding them around)? Moreover, fossilized dinosaur prints have been found in the same rock layers as hoofprints and human footprints. How are we supposed to explain this within the framework of the conventional perspective? And why is it that ancient cultures from every inhabited continent on the planet record interactions with giant reptiles? These creatures are commonly known to us today as *"dragons"* and have been collectively relegated to mythology.

But we must ask ourselves, how is it that so many isolated

cultures from around the world came to share the same mythology so universally? Could there be a core historical truth to the legends? Could it be that the giant reptiles we find buried in the dirt have something to do with the giant reptiles our ancestors spoke of just centuries ago? We believe that this is the case. The preponderance of evidence suggests to us that the conventional perspective is fundamentally flawed. Mankind appears to have collective amnesia regarding this matter, and we have effectively constituted a *"scientific"* paradigm to keep us in the dark.

How then do we account for the extinction of the dinosaurs? The same way we account for the extinction of the other estimated 20,000 to 2 million species which scientists believe may have gone extinct over the past century alone—a combination of climate change and the proliferation of the human species. Climatic change can be very destructive to ecosystems in general, and we tend to kill or drive out all of the major competition in particular. That is why we don't find too many other predators—lions, tigers and bears, etc—in our suburbs and cities, or even our rural communities. We are at the very top of the food chain for a reason.

In Hollywood movies like Jurassic Park we see creatures like Tyrannosaurus rex and velociraptors hunting us down and eating us alive. And, no doubt, if humans and dinosaurs coexisted, some of that certainly happened. But, for the most part, the opposite was true. We hunted them down and cooked them for dinner. In many of the legends and much of the ancient artwork that is exactly what we find—humans hunting down the giant reptiles and killing them. Lions and tigers and bears did not have it quite as bad as the dinosaurs (hence, they are still around). That is because our ancestors seemed particularly fixated on *"slaying the dragon"!*

So, what happened to the dinosaurs? Apparently, the ones that survived global climatic change got eaten by us. Some may still survive in remote areas of the world which have not yet come under our complete dominion, and there are hundreds of such sightings every year to this effect—especially from indigenous, primitive people groups in remote areas who speak to incredulous Western scientists (who naturally do not believe the natives because of their own entrenched, so-called *"scientific"* presuppositions). In our view, this incredulity is wrong. Science should involve the impartial investigation of evidence without prejudice, not an arbitrary human effort to prop up flawed theoretical histories of the earth.

47. QUESTION:
"Why is Biblical Creationism so important?"

ANSWER: Asking why biblical creationism is important is like asking why a foundation is important to a building. Biblical creationism is foundational to the Christian faith. Christianity is established in the book of Genesis chapter one, with *"in the beginning God created . . ."* This one statement affirms creationism and opposes any view that embraces evolutionism (the belief that the universe started with a "big bang" and has been constantly evolving ever since). The way we answer this question reflects whether we believe the Word of God or call its truthfulness into question. As Christians, we must differentiate between creationism and evolutionism; i.e. how are they different, which one is true, and as Christians, come to terms with whether it is possible to believe in both. Those questions can be answered by defining what biblical creationism is and how it affects our fundamental belief system.

The importance of biblica creationism is that it answers the fundamental questions of human existence. 1. How did we get here? Where did we come from? 2. Why are we here? Do we have a purpose, and what is the cause of all or our problems? Are the issues of sin and salvation important? 3. What happens to us when we die? Is there life after death? Genesis is the foundation for the rest of Scripture in which these questions are answered. Genesis has been likened to the root of a tree in that it is the spiritual life-blood of Scripture. If you cut the root from a tree, it dies. If you discredit Genesis, you remove the authoritative value of all Scripture.

Genesis 1:1, *"In the beginning, God created the heavens and the earth,"* gives us three great truths which are the foundations of biblical creationism and the Christian faith. First, we learn of the oneness of God. This stands in contrast to the polytheism and dualism of modern humanist philosophy. Second, we learn of the personality and attributes of God in contrast to pantheism, where God is imminent in the world but is not transcendent to the world. Last, we learn of the omnipotence of God in contrast to the idols that modern humanists hang on to and worship. This one verse tells us that God is eternal—He was before, is now, and always will be—and that He created all that is out of nothing by His spoken word. This answers our creation question of beginnings, but what about our second question, why are we here?

Biblical creationism and the Genesis narrative answer the question of the condition of the human race. It deals with the fall of man but also leaves us with the hope of redemption. It is important that we understand we are unified in one man, Adam—a literal, real-life person. If Adam is not a literal person, then we have no plausible explanation for how sin entered into the world. If mankind did not fall from grace by Adam, then mankind cannot be saved by grace through Jesus Christ. First Corinthians 15:22 (NKJV): *"For as in Adam all die, even so in Christ all shall be made alive."* This parallel of Adam as head of the fallen race and Christ as head of a redeemed race is important to our understanding of the salvation process, and it is essential to understanding its efficacy. *"Therefore, as through one man's offense judgment came to all men, resulting in condemnation, even so through one Man's righteous act the free gift came to all men, resulting in justification of life. For as by one man's disobedience many were made sinners, so also by one Man's obedience many will be made righteous"* Romans 5:18-19 (NKJV).

Considering this, we must then look upon biblical creationism as not only the basis for our value system, but we must look at the creation narrative as factual and not just a story, for if it is a fictional story, then the values it imports are man-reasoned, subject to change as man *"evolves,"* and therefore invalid. This is the basis of the conflict between science and religion (especially Christianity), that science is fact and religion is philosophy. If this is true, then our Christian values are just that, values for Christians, but they have no relevance in the secular world.

The last question for mankind is what happens to us when we die? If man is merely part of the evolved universe and returns to the dirt of the ground when he dies, we must contend that we have no soul or spirit and this life is all there is. This belief leaves us with only one purpose in life, that is following the plan of evolution—survival of the fittest. Christianity, on the other hand, presents us with a moral good that has been established by a higher, transcendent, supernatural Being. The morality of God sets an unchanging standard that not only promotes a better life for us personally, but teaches us how to love others and ultimately bring glory to God, which is our highest calling. This standard is exemplified by the life and work of Christ on the cross. It is through His life, death, and resurrection that we find purpose for this life and hope of a future life with God in heaven.

Biblical creationism is important because it is the only system that answers the basic questions of life and gives us significance greater than ourselves to live for and by. It should be clear to all Christians that we cannot believe in both systems as being true; they are mutually exclusive, and stand in opposition to one another.

48. QUESTION:
"What is the theory of directed panspermia?"

ANSWER: Directed panspermia is a speculative hypothesis about the origin of life on Earth. This hypothesis is a very specific sub-division of a broad group of related ideas. *"Exogenesis"* is a term referring to the general hypothesis that earth life originated somewhere other than Earth, such as another planet. Panspermia, correctly applied, refers to the hypothesis that life existed in some basic form elsewhere in the universe and was spread to Earth and/or some other planets. Directed panspermia is even more specific, proposing that these basic forms, or *"life-seeds,"* were deliberately spread in all directions by some advanced alien race in an effort to begin life wherever they may have landed.

One early promoter of directed panspermia was Francis Crick, one of the co-discoverers of DNA. A committed atheist, Crick once resigned from a collegiate position because the college elected to build a chapel. Crick found his belief in an undesigned, naturally-controlled universe challenged by his discoveries. In particular, Crick found it impossible to believe that DNA could have evolved, based on his knowledge of its structure and the principles of naturalistic evolution. Rather than consider the possibility of DNA being the deliberate construction of an intelligent Creator, Crick mused about ideas like exogenesis, panspermia, and directed panspermia. Crick has since re-affirmed his commitment to the evolution of life on earth from purely natural mechanisms, though with significant questions left unanswered.

Directed panspermia—as well as the more general ideas

of panspermia and exogenesis—are not well accepted in the scientific community. Some see these ideas as semi-contradictory to naturalistic evolution. In reality, the question of how life began on earth is different from the question of how that life progressed. The preferred belief about the origin of earth life is that of abiogenesis (the supposed development of living organisms from non-living matter, also called spontaneous generation), for several reasons. The most overt of these is a lack of evidence suggesting that exogenesis of any kind is likely. Second, a pre-commitment to naturalism is threatened by any suggestion that life might have anything other than a natural origin. Questions about life originating elsewhere raise additional questions about designed or created life, which is not a comfortable topic in naturalistic circles.

Directed panspermia is one of the many strange hypotheses that have been suggested to explain the origins of life on Earth. Even naturalistic science has realized that the question of life's origin is far from answered. While speculation on the evidence supporting evolution rages on, there is little, if any, accepted support for life beginning naturally in the first place. To have life with no God, naturalism has to answer the riddle of abiogenesis, a concept thoroughly refuted by everything known in biology.

Ideas like exogenesis and panspermia are side effects of an attempt to rationalize belief in a universe devoid of God.

The Bible, on the other hand, is God's Word to humanity in which He reveals Himself and His creation of the universe. *"In the beginning, God created the heavens and the earth"* (Genesis 1:1). In this one sentence is everything needed to satisfy completely the basic principles of natural science, the science of foundational things. Natural science deals with a matrix when referring to the material universe. For the complete matrix, you have to have matter, force, energy, space and time. Those five things are all in Genesis 1:1, *"In the beginning [time] God [force] created [energy] the heavens [space] and the earth [matter]."* The complete matrix is in Genesis 1:1 and that is a profound scientific statement. The universe is a matrix of space, time, matter, and energy. And all of it has to be existing at the same conflux. It all has to come together or none of it exists. One cannot exist without the other. The entire continuum must have existed simultaneously from the beginning. That is why you find it all in Genesis 1:1. It all had to be there. Science says it has to be there and Scripture says it is there. The theories of exogenesis, abiogenesis, and panspermia are simply wrong. Theories and philosophies come and go, but the Word of our God is true, trustworthy, right, and perfect, and it stands forever (1 Peter 1:25).

49. QUESTION:
"What are Y-Chromosomal Adam and Mitochondrial Eve?"

ANSWER: *"Y-Chromosomal Adam"* and *"Mitochondrial Eve"* are the scientifically-proven theories that every man alive today is descended from a single man and every man and woman alive today is descended from a single woman.

Humans have 23 pairs of chromosomes. One of those pairs, known as the sex chromosomes (because they determine gender), consists of two X chromosomes in females, and one X-chromosome and one Y-chromosome in males. Girls receive one of their X-chromosomes from their mother and the other from their father. Boys receive the X only from their mother and the Y only from their father. Therefore, the Y-chromosome is passed directly from father to son. Because of this, scientists are able to trace male ancestry.

In 1995, the journal Science published the results of a study in which a segment of the human Y-chromosome from 38 men from different ethnic groups were analyzed for variation (Dorit, R.L., Akashi, H. and Gilbert, W. 1995. *"Absence of polymorphism at the ZFY locus on the human Y chromosome."* Science 268:1183–1185). The segment of the Y-chromosome consisted of 729 base pairs. To their surprise, the researchers found no variation at all. Their conclusion was that the human race must have experienced a genetic bottleneck sometime in the not-too-distant past. Further research was done, and it was determined that every man alive today actually descended from a single man whom scientists now refer to as *"Y-Chromosomal Adam."*

Mitochondrial Eve takes it a step further. While Y-chromosomes are only passed down from father to son, mitochondrial-DNA is passed down from mother to both daughter and son. Because mitochondrial-DNA is only passed on by the mother and never the father, mitochondrial-DNA lineage is the same as maternal lineage. Knowing this, scientists have found that every human alive today can trace their ancestry back to a single woman whom they now refer to as *"Mitochondrial Eve."* While Y-Chromosomal Adam is believed to be the ancestor of every living man, Mitochondrial Eve is believed to be the mother of all living humans, male and female.

It is important to note that this does not prove that Y-Chromosomal Adam was the only man alive before he started having children. This only proves that his descendents are the only ones to have survived. Likewise, Mitochondrial Eve was not necessarily the only woman alive before having children. Rather, all we know for sure is that she is at least one of the ancestors of all living humans. While contemporaries of hers may or may not figure into the ancestry of living humans, we can at least say that none of their mitochondrial-DNA has survived.

Scientists who share the Darwinian bias naturally presume that these two were not the only humans alive during their pre-child bearing lifetimes, while biblical creationists naturally presume that they were. As for determining when these two actually lived respectively, the conventional perspective is founded upon uniformitarian assumptions which many creationists reject, and with fair reason. So there is disagreement there, too. Naturally, the Darwinian time frame is much longer (tens to hundreds of thousands of years), presuming an Old-Earth scenario, while the Young-Earth perspective is much shorter (less than ten thousand years). What we can say with fair certainty is that, regardless of time frames and alleged contemporaries, every man alive today descended from one man while every human alive today descended from one woman.

"Adam named his wife Eve, because she would become the mother of all the living" (Genesis 3:20 NIV).

50. QUESTION:
"What is the difference between Microevolution and Macroevolution?"

ANSWER: Microevolution is an uncontroversial, well-documented, naturally occurring biological phenomenon. It happens every day. It is the process whereby preexisting genetic information is rearranged, corrupted, and/or lost through sexual reproduction and/or genetic mutation producing relatively small-scale (*"micro"*) changes within a population. Two long-haired dogs producing a short-haired puppy would be an example of microevolution (we'll look at why in a moment).

Macroevolution is the somewhat more controversial,

theoretical extrapolation of microevolution that requires the introduction of new genetic information. It is believed to produce large-scale ("macro") changes. An amphibian evolving into a reptile or a reptile evolving into a bird would be examples of macroevolution.

Macroevolution is an important concept because Darwinists believe that it is the mechanism for their idea that all life evolved from a common primordial ancestor. Since microevolution is small-scale (*"micro"*) biological change, and macroevolution is large-scale (*"macro"*) biological change, many Darwinists argue that macroevolution is simply the accumulation of microevolutionary changes over time. Ostensibly, this is a reasonable extrapolation of microevolution. Darwinists, therefore, often cite evidence for microevolution as evidence for macroevolution. However, because macroevolution requires new additional genetic information, no amount of rearrangement, corruption or loss of existing genetic information will produce macroevolution. In other words, no amount of microevolution will produce macroevolution. Darwinists draw a false correlation between the two. We will now take a closer look at both microevolution and macroevoltion.

Microevolution

We will begin with microevolution. Let's say, for example, that within the dog genome there are both a gene for long hair (H) and a gene for short hair (h). Now imagine that the very first dogs possessed both genes (Hh). If two Hh dogs bred, half of the Hh from one dog would combine with half of the Hh from the other dog through sexual reproduction, and there would be four possible outcomes for offspring: HH, Hh, hH and hh puppies.

Now let's suppose that the longhair H gene is the dominant gene and the shorthair h gene is the recessive gene. That means that when a dog possesses both genes, only the longhair H gene will be expressed, i.e., the dog will have long hair. So, if two longhair Hh dogs bred, the odds are that they would have three longhair puppies (HH, Hh and hH) and one shorthair puppy (hh). The two longhair dogs having a shorthair puppy would be an example of change within a population resulting from the rearrangement of preexisting genetic information (i.e., microevolution).

If longhair Hh dog bred with a shorthair hh dog, the odds are that they would have two longhair puppies (Hh and hH) and two shorthair puppies (hh and hh). If two shorthair hh dogs bred, they would produce only shorthair hh puppies. And if this group of shorthair hh dogs became isolated from the longhair HH, Hh and hH dogs, they would lose access to the longhair H gene altogether and become an *"isolated gene pool."* When it comes to dogs, isolated gene pools are called *"purebreds."* Likewise, if a group of longhair HH dogs became isolated from the shorthair h gene, they would be considered purebred. On the other hand, the longhair Hh and hH dogs would be called *"mutts."* Human breeders have been exploiting this biological phenomenon for thousands of years, selecting dog couples to mate based on their appearance in order to accentuate and attenuate traits gradually over time and thereby introduce new breeds

GENETIC MUTATION

Now imagine that, within a longhair Hh population, a genetic mutation disabled the expression of the longhair H gene, and that mutation was reproduced over and over again within the population. The formerly longhair population would become shorthair, not because of the rearrangement of genes through sexual reproduction but because of genetic mutation.

Another important example of microevolution through genetic mutation is when a population of insects becomes resistant to a certain pesticide, or when bacteria become resistant to antibiotics. What happens in these instances is that through mutation the insects or bacteria lose the ability to produce the enzyme which interacts with the poison. The pesticide or antibiotic, therefore, has no effect. But the insects or bacteria don't gain any new genetic information; they lose it. It is not, therefore, an example of macroevolution as it is often misinterpreted, but of microevolution. As biophysicist Dr. Lee Spetner explains, *"All of the mutations that have been examined on a molecular level show that the organism has lost information and not gained it."* (*"From a Frog to a Prince,"* documentary by Keziah Films, 1998)

MACROEVOLUTION

Now let's look at macroevolution. Darwinists believe that all life is genetically related and has descended from a common ancestor. The first birds and the first mammals are believed to have evolved from a reptile; the first reptile is believed to have evolved from an amphibian; the first amphibian is believed to have evolved from a fish; the first fish is believed to have evolved from a lower form of life, and so on, until we go all the way back to the first single-celled organism, which is believed to have evolved from inorganic matter. [The acronym to remember is FARM: Fish to Amphibian to Reptile to Mammal.]

The very first single-celled organism did not possess all of the genetic information for a human, so in order for humans to have ultimately evolved from a primitive single-celled organism, a lot of genetic information had to be added along the way. Change resulting from the introduction of new genetic information is *"macroevolution."*

The reason why macroevolution is controversial and remains theoretical is that there is no known way for entirely new genetic information to be added to a genome. Darwinists have been hoping that genetic mutation would provide a mechanism, but so far that has not been the case. As Dr. Spetner again explains, *"I really do not believe that the neo-Darwinian model can account for large-scale evolution [i.e., macroevolution]. What they really can't account for is the buildup of information. ...And not only is it improbable on the mathematical level, that is, theoretically, but experimentally one has not found a single mutation that one can point at that actually adds information. In fact, every beneficial mutation that I have seen reduces the information, it loses information."* (Ibid.)

CREATION VS. EVOLUTION

When Creationists say they don't believe in evolution, they are not talking about microevolution. They are referring to macroevolution. Microevolution is a credibly observed scientific phenomenon. What Creationists do not believe in is Darwin's macroevolutionary extrapolation of microevolution. Unlike microevolution, there is no true scientific evidence for macroevolution, and, in fact, there is significant evidence against it. The distinction between microevolution and macroevolution is, therefore, an important one for those interested in the creation-vs.-evolution debate.

51. QUESTION:
"How is Intelligent Design any different from belief in a Flying Spaghetti Monster?"

ANSWER: In 2005, in protest of the Kansas State Board of Education's decision to require the teaching of Intelligent Design in addition to Darwinian evolution, Bobby Henderson professed belief in a Flying Spaghetti Monster as the universe's supernatural creator. Henderson then mockingly demanded that his belief that the Flying Spaghetti Monster (also known as the Spaghedeity) created the universe with a touch from his *"noodly appendage."* With the motive of mocking the Intelligent Design Theory, Henderson wrote, *"I think we can all look forward to the time when these three theories are given equal time in our science classrooms across the country, and eventually the world—one-third time for Intelligent Design, one-third time for Flying Spaghetti Monsterism, and one-third time for logical conjecture based on overwhelming observable evidence."*

From this beginning, Flying Spaghetti Monsterism has gained a *"cult"* following, with its advocates calling themselves *"Pastafarians."* None of the advocates of Pastafarianism genuinely believes in the existence of the Flying Spaghetti Monster. Rather, this mock religion's only intent is to argue against Intelligent Design being taught in schools as an alternative theory to Darwinian evolution. Pastafarians claim that if Intelligent Design is taught in schools, then every conceivable theory of origins must be taught as well. This would obviously result in confusion and chaos.

So, do Pastafarians have a point? Does the idea of a Flying Spaghetti Monster illustrate how foolish it is to try to bring religion into the classroom? The answer is a resounding no. The entire concept of Flying Spaghetti Monsterism / Pastafarianism is built on a faulty premise—that the Intelligent Design Theory is the same thing as literal biblical creationism. Anyone who has truly examined the writings of Intelligent Design advocates realizes this fact. Granted, there are some who are using the Intelligent Design Theory to attempt to force literal biblical creationism into science classrooms, but that is not what the Intelligent Design theory is at its core.

The Intelligent Design Theory—that the vast majority of its advocates are trying to get into the science classrooms—is the idea that biological life exhibits such extraordinary complexity that it could not have come to be entirely in a naturalistic vacuum. The more that science advances, the more obvious it becomes that the universe and the life that is within it could not be the result of completely random, unguided, and non-designed chance. This understanding of the Intelligent Design Theory is clearly not the same as literal biblical creationism. In fact, Intelligent Design is no more an argument for biblical creationism than it is an argument for theistic evolution.

While the advocates of Flying Spaghetti Monsterism are entertaining, creative, and excellent at satire, the system fails in that it is an argument against only an extreme minority within the Intelligent Design movement. Pastafarianism does not apply, or in any way refute, the core arguments of the Intelligent Design Theory. The question of which implication of the Intelligent Design Theory is correct is a subject far better suited to philosophy / theology classrooms than science classrooms. The Intelligent Design Theory itself, however, is a valid issue to be raised within the science classroom, due to naturalistic science's failure to demonstrate how the universe, and life within the universe, came into existence without the intervention of an Intelligent Designer.

52. QUESTION:
"What is the theory of abiogenesis? What is the definition of abiogenesis?"

ANSWER: Abiogenesis is the idea of life originating from non-living material (non-life). This concept has expanded a great deal as mankind's understanding of science has grown, but all forms of abiogenesis have one thing in common: they are all scientifically unsupportable. There have been no experiments demonstrating abiogenesis in action. It has never been observed in a natural or artificial environment. Conditions believed to have existed on earth are either incapable of producing the building blocks needed, or self-contradictory. No evidence has been found suggesting where or when such life might have generated. In fact, everything we know of science today seems to indicate that abiogenesis could not have happened under any naturally possible conditions.

Early concepts of abiogenesis were very simplistic. Rotting meat was soon covered in maggots, and so it was assumed that the meat turned into maggots. Mice were usually seen in places where hay was stored, so it was assumed that hay turned into mice. This type of abiogenesis is known as *"spontaneous generation.*" This was actually the popular scientific explanation for the reproduction of living things as recently as a few hundred years ago. It wasn't until the mid-1800s that men like Pasteur proved experimentally that living things can only come from other living things. That is, science eventually proved conclusively that the only supportable origin for any living cell is another living cell.

Modern ideas of abiogenesis can be very complex, and some are more outrageously unlikely than others. Guesses are widely varied, from deep-sea lava vents to meteoric impact sites and even radioactive beaches. In general, all modern theories of abiogenesis imagine some scenario in which natural conditions create, combine, and arrange molecules in such a way that they begin to self-replicate. These theories vary widely as to the nature of these conditions, the complexity of the molecules, and so forth. All share at least one common factor: they are implausible to the point of impossibility, based on established science.

One problem with modern abiogenesis is the extraordinary complexity of living organisms. Experiments have proven that very simple amino acids can be formed in laboratory conditions. However, these separate acids are nowhere near sufficient to create a living cell. The conditions which create these acids would not only kill any such cell as soon as it was formed, but are also unlikely to have ever actually existed at any time in earth's history. Any evolutionary theory that seems to suggest how ultra-simple life could have developed from a single newly formed cell has no answer for how that cell could have been formed in the first place. There is no *"prototype first cell."* Science has never even come close to producing a self-sustaining living cell that could have been produced by, or survived in, the conditions needed to form its components.

It has been said that *"death is philosophy's only problem."* This may or may not be true, but dealing with death presents a major challenge to any philosophical view. In much the same way, abiogenesis is the scientific naturalist's biggest problem. There are naturalistic guesses about how life could have begun without any Creator or Designer. And yet, these purely natural explanations are thoroughly refuted by science itself. It is ironic that so many people proclaim scientific naturalism to be *"proven," "established,"* or *"demonstrated"* so clearly. And yet, naturalism is necessarily linked to abiogenesis, which is scientifically impossible.

The overwhelming evidence that life cannot come from non-life is a powerful indication that naturalism is not a realistic worldview. Life either had a natural origin (abiogenesis) or a supernatural origin (intelligent design). The scientific impossibility of abiogenesis is an argument for, at least, a supernatural originator. The only way to create even the most basic building blocks of life is in non-natural, highly designed, and tightly controlled conditions. That, by itself, makes it reasonable to presume that life cannot begin without intelligent intervention.

53. QUESTION:
"What is the theory of punctuated equilibrium?"

ANSWER: *"Punctuated equilibrium"* refers to a concept in evolutionary biology that is both controversial and widely misunderstood. Both punctuated equilibrium and its alternatives have significant drawbacks, either in plausibility or evidence. Punctuated equilibrium seeks to reconcile the idea of natural evolution with the missing links in the fossil record. The debate within science over the validity of punctuated equilibrium demonstrates many of the problems with evolutionary theory in general.

Punctuated equilibrium attempts to answer a major problem with the fossil record. For almost a century, naturalistic science assumed that the gaps in the fossil record would eventually be filled, and there would be a semi-complete record of so-called *"transitional forms"* between the various species. In fact, the opposite happened, and the gaps became even more pronounced. The actual fossil record indicates species seemingly appearing from nowhere, and without the long, slow, gradual changes expected by classical evolutionary theory. Punctuated equilibrium seeks to answer this problem by supposing that evolution doesn't occur steadily, but sporadically.

In 1972, Stephen Gould and Niles Eldredge published a landmark paper on punctuated equilibrium. Their contention was that the gaps in the fossil record were best explained by gaps in evolution. That is, that most species did not change much over time, but occasionally experienced major changes in brief periods of time. *"Classic"* Darwinian evolution is presumed to take place very gradually, with a steady and slow change of organisms over time. Punctuated equilibrium replaces this slow change with long periods lacking any change at all, mixed with relatively short periods of rapid change.

Another way of looking at this is to say that, according to punctuated equilibrium, species are normally not evolving, and when they do evolve, it is relatively quick and dramatic. At times, this has become a source of controversy within the scientific community. Depending on whom you ask, punctuated equilibrium is either a refutation of gradual evolution, or just a specific form of it. This is one of the major disagreements over the theory—whether it replaces or enhances the classical notion of naturalistic evolution.

Despite a better agreement with available evidence, there are many scientific problems with punctuated equilibrium itself. The mechanism for punctuated equilibrium is assumed to be small groups of a particular organism separated in some way from the main population. This would accelerate the transmission of mutated genes through the population, and much more quickly produce a new species. However, multiple studies have found that inbreeding such as this produces extremely negative effects, which run counter to the idea of rapid advancement. The fossil record also calls into question the plausibility of this notion. The so-called *"Cambrian Explosion,"* for instance, is the sudden emergence of almost every biological type known to man, in a geological blink of an eye. This seems to contradict the idea of broad genetic stability intermixed with localized change.

There are also several points of irony related to punctuated equilibrium that have little to do with the science, and a great deal to do with the assumptions of the scientists. Gould was criticized for being heavy on rhetoric and light on scientific substance by the *"old guard"* of evolutionary theory. This same criticism has been applied by theists to atheistic naturalism in general. Gould and Eldredge predicted resistance to their ideas, stating that the scientific community was too devoted to theories and not facts. That is, they expected to be resisted for no other reason than what they proposed didn't follow the preferred assumptions. More than 30 years later, this is still one of the major obstacles to open, honest dialogue about science.

Punctuated equilibrium represents an odd combination of traits. It closes some holes in evolutionary theory, but opens up others. It supposedly makes evolutionary theory more evidence-based, and therefore more scientific, but it also makes the *"naturalism of the gaps"* attitude easier to take. That is, punctuated equilibrium makes it easier to explain away the lack of transitional forms as though it was evidence that actually supports evolution.

When all is said and done, punctuated equilibrium is an attempt to reconcile available evidence with the idea of naturalistic evolution. It is, in many ways, another example of re-interpreting facts in order to fit an ideology. Still, any willingness to modify evolutionary theory in light of evidence is good, since this can only lead closer and closer to the idea of a Creator God. Pursuit of these ideas might help close the philosophical gaps between atheistic naturalism and intelligent design—which might be the very reason punctuated equilibrium is so highly resisted in some academic circles.

54. QUESTION:
"Does the Bible teach that the earth is flat?"

ANSWER: Many a skeptic claims that the Bible depicts a flat earth. Scriptural references such as Revelation 7:1 are cited, which speaks of *"four angels standing at the four corners of the earth."* However, this passage makes reference to the cardinal directions as seen on a compass—i.e. north, south, east and west. Terminology to a similar effect is used today when we speak of the sun rising and setting each day, even though we know that it is, in fact, the earth which orbits around the sun.

Another passage often referred to is Psalm 75:3, which speaks of God holding the pillars firm. However, the psalms are written in the poetry genre. Rather than referring to literal pillars, this is representative of God's guaranteeing the earth's stability. Even when the moral order of the world seems to have crumbled, God will not fully withdraw His sustaining power.

In contrast to the supposed *"flat earth"* verses, there are numerous Scriptures that clearly indicate otherwise. The earth is described in Job 26:7 as being suspended over empty space, implying a spherical figure. This notion is further entertained in Isaiah 40:21-22, which refers to *"the circle of the earth."* This is further supported by Proverbs 8:27 (NKJV), which speaks of God drawing a circle on the face of the deep. From a *"bird's-eye view"* of the ocean, the horizon is seen as a circle. Such an observation indicates that where light terminates, darkness begins, describing the reality of day and night on a spherical earth.

The round-earth idea is further supported by Jesus in Luke 17:31,34: *"In that day, he who is on the housetop, and his goods are in the house, let him not come down to take them away. And likewise the one who is in the field, let him not turn back...I tell you, in that night there will be two people in one bed: the one will be taken and the other will be left."* This would seem to indicate the phenomenon of day on one side of the globe while darkness abides on the other.

In conclusion, the curvature of the earth is certainly a biblical concept, and there is little or no basis for the charge that the Bible teaches a flat earth. The Scriptures that seem to present a flat earth can all easily be explained when correctly interpreted and understood.

55. QUESTION:
"What is the God particle?"

ANSWER: The *"God particle"* is the nickname of a subatomic particle called the Higgs boson. In layman's terms, different subatomic particles are responsible for giving matter different properties. One of the most mysterious and important properties is mass. Some particles, like protons and neutrons, have mass. Others, like photons, do not. The Higgs boson, or *"God particle,"* is believed to be the particle which gives mass to matter. The *"God particle"* nickname grew out of the long, drawn-out struggles of physicists to find this elusive piece of the cosmic puzzle. What follows is a very brief, very simplified explanation of how the Higgs boson fits into modern physics, and how science is attempting to study it.

The *"standard model"* of particle physics is a system that attempts to describe the forces, components, and reactions of the basic particles that make up matter. It not only deals with atoms and their components, but the pieces that compose some subatomic particles. This model does have some major gaps, including gravity, and some experimental contradictions. The standard model is still a very good method of understanding particle physics, and it continues to improve. The model predicts that there are certain elementary particles even smaller than protons and neutrons. As of the date of this writing, the only particle predicted by the model which has not been experimentally verified is the *"Higgs boson,"* jokingly referred to as the *"God particle."*

Each of the subatomic particles contributes to the forces that cause all matter interactions. One of the most important, but least understood, aspects of matter is mass. Science is not entirely sure why some particles seem mass-less, like photons, and others are *"massive."* The standard model predicts that there is an elementary particle, the Higgs boson, which would produce the effect of mass. Confirmation of the Higgs boson would be a major milestone in our understanding of physics.

The *"God particle"* nickname actually arose when the book The God Particle: If the Universe Is the Answer, What Is the Question? by Leon Lederman was published. Since then, it's taken on a life of its own, in part because of the monumental questions about matter that the God particle might be able to answer. The man who first proposed the Higgs boson's existence, Peter Higgs, isn't all that amused by the nickname

"*God particle*," as he's an avowed atheist. All the same, there isn't really any religious intention behind the nickname.

Currently, efforts are under way to confirm the Higgs boson using the Large Hadron Collider, a particle accelerator in Switzerland, which should be able to confirm or refute the existence of the God particle. As with any scientific discovery, God's amazing creation becomes more and more impressive as we learn more about it. Either result—that the Higgs boson exists, or does not exist—represents a step forward in human knowledge and another step forward in our appreciation of God's awe-inspiring universe. Whether or not there is a "*God particle*," we know this about Christ: "*For by him all things were created: things in heaven and on earth, visible and invisible . . . all things were created by him and for him*" (Colossians 1:16).

56. QUESTION:
"What is the God of the gaps argument?"

ANSWER: The *"God-of-the-gaps"* argument refers to a perception of the universe in which anything that currently can be explained by our knowledge of natural phenomena is considered outside the realm of divine interaction, and thus the concept of *"God"* is invoked to explain what science is, as yet, incapable of explaining. In other words, only the *"gaps"* in scientific knowledge are explained by the work of God, hence the name *"God of the gaps."*

The idea is that as scientific research progresses, and an increasing number of phenomena are explained naturalistically, the role of God diminishes accordingly. The major criticism commonly states that invoking supernatural explanations should decrease in plausibility over time, as the domain of knowledge previously explained by God is decreasing.

However, with modern advances in science and technology, the tables have been literally turned. With the advent of electron scanning microscopes, we have been able to observe the intricate workings of the cell for the first time. What had originally and simplistically been thought to be nothing more than a "blob" of protoplasm is now seen to be far more complex and information-packed than had ever been conceived of previously.

Much of what had once been filed away as *"solved"* in the early twentieth century is now found to be inadequately explained by naturalism. Twenty-first century technology is increasingly revealing gaping holes in conventional evolutionary theory. The information-rich content of the *"simple"* has only recently been understood at any real level and found to be anything but simple. Information can now be understood to be inherently non-material. Therefore, materialistic processes cannot qualify as sources of information.

In reality, a belief in God can be derived by means of an objective assessment, rather than the subjective conjecture that may have been the case millennia ago. But many people simply deny what is obvious to them. The Bible addresses those very people: *"The wrath of God is being revealed from heaven against all the godlessness and wickedness of men who suppress the truth by their wickedness, since what may be known about God is plain to them, because God has made it plain to them. For since the creation of the world God's invisible qualities—his eternal power and divine nature—have been clearly seen, being understood from what has been made, so that men are without excuse"* (Romans 1:18-20). The God-of-the-gaps argument is an example of *"suppressing the truth"* because it relegates God to a *"backup"* explanation for those things which cannot yet be explained by natural phenomena. This leads some to the faulty conclusion that God is not the omnipotent, omnipresent, absolute Being of whom Scripture testifies.

There is much for which the natural sciences simply cannot provide an explanation, such as the origin of the time/space/matter continuum and the fine-tuning thereof; the origin and subsequent development of life itself; and the origin of the complex and specified information systems inherent in all living things, which cannot (nor ever will be) explained by natural means. Thus one cannot rationally divorce the supernatural from the observed universe, proving once again that *"in the beginning God created the heavens and the earth"* (Genesis 1:1).

57. Question:
"What are some flaws in the theory of evolution?"

Answer: Christians and non-Christians alike often question whether the theory of evolution is accurate. Those who express doubts about the theory are often labeled "unscientific" or *"backwards"* by some in the pro-evolution camp. At times, the popular perception of evolution seems to be that it has been proven beyond all doubt and there are no scientific obstacles left for it. In reality, there are quite a few scientific flaws in the theory that provide reasons to be skeptical. Granted, none of these questions necessarily disproves evolution, but they do show how the theory is less than settled.

There are many ways in which evolution can be criticized scientifically, but most of those criticisms are highly specific. There are countless examples of genetic characteristics, ecological systems, evolutionary trees, enzyme properties, and other facts that are very difficult to square with the theory of evolution. Detailed descriptions of these can be highly technical and are beyond the scope of a summary such as this. Generally speaking, it's accurate to say that science has yet to provide consistent answers to how evolution operates at the molecular, genetic, or even ecological levels in a consistent and supportable way.

Other flaws in the theory of evolution can be separated into three basic areas. First, there is the contradiction between *"punctuated equilibrium"* and *"gradualism."* Second is the problem in projecting *"microevolution"* into *"macroevolution."* Third is the unfortunate way in which the theory has been unscientifically abused for philosophical reasons.

First, there is a contradiction between *"punctuated equilibrium"* and *"gradualism."* There are two basic possibilities for how naturalistic evolution can occur. This flaw in the theory of evolution occurs because these two ideas are mutually exclusive, and yet there is evidence suggestive of both of them. Gradualism implies that organisms experience a relatively steady rate of mutations, resulting in a somewhat *"smooth"* transition from early forms to later ones. This was the original assumption derived from the theory of evolution. Punctuated equilibrium, on the other hand, implies that mutation rates are heavily influenced by a unique set of coincidences. Therefore, organisms will experience long periods of stability, *"punctuated"* by short bursts of rapid evolution.

Gradualism seems to be contradicted by the fossil record. Organisms appear suddenly and demonstrate little change over long periods. The fossil record has been greatly expanded over the last century, and the more fossils that are found, the more gradualism seems to be disproved. It was this overt refutation of gradualism in the fossil record that prompted the theory of punctuated equilibrium.

The fossil record might seem to support punctuated equilibrium, but again, there are major problems. The basic assumption of punctuated equilibrium is that a very few creatures, all from the same large population, will experience several beneficial mutations, all at the same time. Right away, one can see how improbable this is. Then, those few members separate completely from the main population so that their new genes can be passed to the next generation (another unlikely event). Given the wide diversity of life, this kind of amazing coincidence would have to happen all the time.

While the improbable nature of punctuated equilibrium speaks for itself, scientific studies have also cast doubt on the benefits it would confer. Separating a few members from a larger population results in inbreeding. This results in decreased reproductive ability, harmful genetic abnormalities, and so forth. In essence, the events that should be promoting *"survival of the fittest"* cripple the organisms instead.

Despite what some claim, punctuated equilibrium is not a more refined version of gradualism. They have very different assumptions about the mechanisms behind evolution and the way those mechanisms behave. Neither is a satisfactory explanation for how life came to be as diverse and balanced as it is, and yet there are no other reasonable options for how evolution can operate.

The second flaw is the problem of extending *"microevolution"* into *"macroevolution."* Laboratory studies have shown that organisms are capable of adaptation. That is, living things have an ability to shift their biology to better fit their environment. However, those same studies have demonstrated that such changes can only go so far, and those organisms have not fundamentally changed. These small changes are called *"microevolution."* Microevolution can result in some drastic changes, such as those found in dogs. All dogs are the same species, and one can see how much variation there is. But even the most aggressive breeding has never turned a dog into something else. There is a limit to how large, small, smart, or hairy a dog can become through breeding. Experimentally, there is no reason to suggest that a species can change beyond its own genetic limits and become something else.

Long-term evolution, though, requires *"macroevolution,"* which refers to those large-scale changes. Microevolution turns a wolf into a Chihuahua or a Great Dane. Macroevolution would turn a fish into a cow or a duck. There is a massive difference in scale and effect between microevolution and macroevolution. This flaw in the theory of evolution is that experimentation does not support the ability of many small changes to transform one species into another.

Finally, there is the flawed application of evolution. This is not a flaw in the scientific theory, of course, but an error in the way the theory has been abused for non-scientific purposes. There are still many, many questions about biological life that evolution has not answered. And yet, there are those who try to transform the theory from a biological explanation into a metaphysical one. Every time a person claims that the theory of evolution disproves religion, spirituality, or God, they are taking the theory outside of its own limits. Fairly or not, the theory of evolution has been hijacked as an anti-religious mascot by those with an axe to grind against God.

Overall, there are many solidly scientific reasons to question the theory of evolution. These flaws may be resolved by science, or they may eventually kill the theory all together. We don't know which one will happen, but we do know this: the theory of evolution is far from settled, and rational people can question it scientifically.

58. Question:
"What is Old Earth Creationism?"

Answer: Old Earth Creationism is an umbrella term used to describe biblical creationists who deny that the universe was created within the last 6,000 to 10,000 years over the course of six consecutive 24-hour days. Rather, Old Earth Creationists believe that God created the universe and its inhabitants (including a literal Adam and Eve) over a much longer period of time than is allowed for by Young Earth Creationists. The list of notable Christian leaders who are at least open to an Old Earth interpretation is a long one and that list continues to grow. The list includes men such as Walter Kaiser, Norman Geisler, William Dembski, J.I. Packer, J.P. Moreland, Philip E. Johnson, and Chuck Colson, as well the late Francis Schaefer and Old Testament scholar Gleason Archer.

Old Earth Creationists usually agree with the mainstream scientific estimates of the age of the universe, humanity, and Earth itself while at the same time rejecting the claims of modern evolutionary theorists with respect to biological evolution. Old Earth Creationists and their Young Earth Creationist brothers hold several important points in common, including

1) The literal creation of the universe out of nothing a finite time ago (creation ex nihilo).

2) The literal creation of Adam out of the dust of the ground and Eve out of Adam's side as well as the historicity of the Genesis account.

3) The rejection of the claim of Darwinists that random

mutation and natural selection can adequately account for the complexity of life.

4) The rejection of the claim that God used the process of evolution to bring man to today (theistic evolution). Both Old Earth and New Earth Creationism categorically reject the theory of common ancestry.

However, Old Earth Creationists differ with Young Earth Creationists on the following:

1) The age of the universe. Young Earth Creationists believe that God created the universe 6,000-10,000 years ago. Old Earth Creationists place the creation event at approximately 13.7 billion years ago, thus being more in line with *"mainstream"* science, at least on this point.

2) The time of the creation of Adam and Eve. Young Earth Creationists place the creation of Adam no later than 10,000 years ago. Old Earth Creationists are varied on this point with estimates ranging somewhere between 30,000-70,000 thousand years ago.

The controversy between the two views of creationism hinges on the meaning of the Hebrew word yom, meaning "day." Young Earth Creationists insist that the meaning of the word yom in the context of Genesis 1–2 is a 24-hour period of time. Old Earth Creationists disagree and believe that the word yom is being used to denote a much longer duration of time. Old Earth Creationists have used numerous biblical arguments to defend their view including the following:

1) Yom is used elsewhere in the Bibl where it is referring to a long period of time, particularly Psalm 90:4, which is later cited by the apostle Peter: *"A day (yom) is like a thousand years"* (2 Peter 3:8).

2) The seventh *"day"* is thousands of years long. Genesis 2:2-3 states that God rested on the seventh *"day"* (yom). Scripture teaches that we are certainly still in the seventh day; therefore, the word *"day"* could also be referring to a long period of time with reference to days one through six.

3) The word *"day"* in Genesis 1–2 is longer than 24 hours. Genesis 2:4 reads, *"This is the account of the heavens and the earth when they were created in the day that the LORD God made*

earth and heaven" (NASB). In this verse, *"day"* is referring to the first six days as a whole and thus has a more flexible meaning than merely a 24-hour period.

4) The sixth *"day"* is probably longer than 24 hours. Genesis 2:19 tells us that Adam observed and then catalogued every living animal on the earth. At face value, it does not appear that Adam could have completed such a monumental task in a mere 24-hour period.

To be sure, the issues dividing Young and Old Earth Creationists are both complex and significant. However, this issue should not be made a test for orthodoxy. There are godly men and women on both sides of this debate. In the final analysis, biblical creationists—both Young and Old Earth varieties—have a great deal in common and should work together to defend the historical reliability of the Genesis account.

59. QUESTION:
"Is the universe eternal?"

ANSWER: The Bible makes it clear that the universe is not eternal, that it had a beginning, and that the beginning was its creation by God (Genesis 1:1). This truth has been denied by philosophers and pseudo-scientists who have come up with a variety of different theories in an effort to *"prove"* the eternality of the universe. Further, atheists will say that matter and energy are eternal, following the first law of thermodynamics— *"Energy can be transformed (changed from one form to another), but it can neither be created nor destroyed."*

Philosophically, why do we have something rather than nothing at all? If the universe had a beginning, then it must have a cause, and therefore cannot be eternal. And every drop of evidence we have points to the universe having a beginning, but this truth is not something welcomed by naturalists and atheists. Numerous scientifically minded atheists have expressed a desire to find a loophole to the scientific fact that the present order of nature had a beginning. Unfortunately for them, such a loophole does not exist. Here are five proofs that the universe is not eternal:

(1) The universe is running down, and something that is running down must have started at some point. The second law of thermodynamics states that the universe is running out of usable energy and if you doubt this, look in the mirror (you're aging and running down just like everything else).

(2) The universe is expanding. This was confirmed through the Hubble telescope many years ago, and it is interesting to note that the universe is expanding from a single point, meaning the entire universe could be contracted back into a single point. Also, note that the universe is not expanding into space, but space itself is expanding.

(3) The radiation echo was discovered by Bell Labs scientists in 1965. What is it? It is the heat afterglow from the Big Bang. Its discovery dealt a death blow to any theory of the universe being in a steady state because it shows instead that the universe exploded.

(4) Galaxy Seeds. Scientists believe that, if the Big Bang is true (first, there was nothing, then, BANG, something came into being), then temperature *"ripples"* should exist in space, and it would be these ripples that enabled matter to collect into

galaxies. To discover whether these ripples exist, the Cosmic Background Explorer—COBE—was launched in 1989 to find them, with the findings being released in 1992. What COBE found was perfect/precise ripples that, sure enough, enable galaxies to form. So critical and spectacular was this finding that the NASA lead for COBE, said, *"If you're religious, it's like looking at God."*

(5) Albert Einstein's theory of relativity means that the universe had a beginning and was not eternal as he had previously believed (Einstein was originally a pantheist). His theory proved that the universe is not a cause, but instead one big effect—something brought it into existence. Einstein disliked his end result so much that he introduced a "fudge factor" into his theory that allowed for an eternal universe. But there was only one problem. His fudge factor required a division by zero in his calculations—a mathematical error any good math student knows not to make. When discovered by other mathematicians, Einstein admitted his error calling it *"the greatest blunder of my life."* After his acknowledgment, and upon confirming further research that showed the universe expanding just as his theory of relativity predicted, Einstein bowed to the fact that the universe is not eternal and said that he wanted *"to know how God created*

the world."

Further, it should be understood that every effect must resemble its cause. This is because, simply put, you cannot give what you do not have, so it is impossible for an effect to possess something its originating cause did not have. That being the case, how can one believe that an impersonal, amoral, purposeless, and meaningless universe accidentally created beings that are full of personality, morals, meaning, and purpose? Only mind can create mind. In the end it is either matter before mind or mind before matter, and all scientific, philosophical, and reasonable evidence points to the latter.

In conclusion, we find that all scientific evidence points to the fact that the universe had a beginning, just as the Bible states, and that a Cause must exist that resembles all we know today. As Lord Kelvin, a British scientist once said, *"If you study science deep enough and long enough, it will force you to believe in God."*

60. QUESTION:
"Why didn't Adam and Eve find it strange that a serpent was talking to them?"

ANSWER: Interestingly, the serpent/snake speaking to Adam and Eve is not the only instance in the Bible where an animal speaks. The prophet Balaam was rebuked by his donkey (see Numbers 22:21-35). We have to remember that while animals are not capable of speaking, there are powerful beings out there (God, the angels, Satan, the demons) who are capable of the impossible, including enabling animals to speak. Most scholars hold that it was Satan in the Garden of Eden who was speaking through the snake, not the snake itself speaking on its own. Thus, the Genesis 3 account it is not suggesting that snakes were of an intellect that would have enabled them to speak coherently.

Still, why didn't Adam and Eve find it strange that an animal was speaking to them? It is unlikely that Adam and Eve had the same perspective we do on animals. In our era, we know from experience that animals are incapable of speech on the same level as humans. Adam and Eve did not have a childhood, nor did they have other humans to learn from. Given that Adam and Eve had probably only been alive a matter of days, it is not unreasonable for them to believe that animals were capable of speech. It is also possible that this was not the first talking animal Adam and Eve had encountered. Perhaps Satan or even God Himself had used animals to communicate with Adam and Eve before. There are so few details given in the account that much is left to speculation and presumption.

Lastly, it was not unreasonable for Eve to answer the snake. After all, the snake was evidently speaking in a language that she understood and asking an intelligible question. It is also likely that Adam was nearby and could verify that she was not imagining things. It was not the serpent speaking that should have alarmed them. Rather, it was the fact that he was causing them to doubt God's instructions (Genesis 3:1), contradicting God (Genesis 3:4), and calling God's motives into question (Genesis 3:5). That should have been enough to cause both Eve and Adam to stop talking to the serpent.

61. QUESTION:
"The Missing Link - has it been found?"

ANSWER: Every so often, news outlets irresponsibly report the sensational claim that someone somewhere has finally found *"the missing link."* This gives people the false impression that some scientist somewhere has, at long last, discovered the fossilized remains of some kind of half-human, half-apelike creature (thereby proving Darwin's theory). In actual fact, no such fossil has ever been found. All that has ever been found are the fossilized remains of prosimians, monkeys, apes and humans. But, eager as they are to find the ever-missing *"missing link"* and lay the controversy to rest, Darwinists tend to hone in on any superficial aspect of a fossil that they could possibly interpret as a mark of evolutionary transition from monkey to ape, or from ape to human, and news organizations are more than happy to print sensational headlines (which, needless to say, are good for business).

Take Darwinius massillae for example, the fossil discovery also known as *"Ida"* (after the daughter of the Norwegian scientist who led the research team). Ida looks exactly like a modern lemur except that she lacks the tooth-comb and grooming-claw common to modern lemurs. Darwinists excitedly interpreted this to mean that she must have been an evolutionary transition from prosimian (the group to which lemurs belong) to monkey, since monkeys don't have tooth-combs or grooming-claws (and neither does Ida). This is not the only possible interpretation, as we shall see, but it suits Darwinists just fine. And it is sensational, of course, which suits the media as well.

Now, what happens if we find a man born with hands but no arms, so that his hands are attached directly to his shoulders? Should we believe that he is evolving into a fish? That would seem to be the same rationale being used here by Darwinists. The fact is there are people born with hands but no arms and they are all still 100% human. They are known as *"phocomeli."* They suffer from *"phocomelia,"* a condition which can either be inherited or caused by prenatal exposure to the drug thalidomide.

Could it be that just as phocomeli suffer from a terrible deformity, so, too, did this fossilized lemur? It is entirely possible. But what would be more sensational to report—the discovery of the fossilized remains of a dead deformed lemur or the finding of an exciting new species that might fit somewhere within the presumed family tree of human evolution? In fact, if we go with the latter instead of the former, people could make outrageous claims like it's *"the eighth wonder of the world..."* Google could incorporate Ida's image into their logo for a day... headlines could proclaim that we've finally found the missing link... and eager Charles Darwin devotees could claim victory once and for all, all of which actually happened with Ida in 2009, all because of one dead lemur with two missing body parts.

The news reports also made a big deal out of the fact that Ida has opposable thumbs and nails instead of claws, which are human characteristics, but they didn't bother to mention that modern lemurs also have opposable thumbs and nails instead of claws, so those features have no evolutionary significance whatsoever.

Unfortunately, this is not an isolated incident. Example after example could be given of mere fragments of bone and even pig's teeth that have been imagined into ape-men, sold to the public and placed in textbooks. Bones of 100% humans have been wrongly categorized with the bones of 100% apes to create non-existent, ape-men species. Diseased human skeletons have been distorted to look more ape-like and put on display. Even the wide range of potential anatomical variations among humans has been misinterpreted, not only among dead human specimens but among living humans as well.

Modern Australian Aborigines, for example, are known for their deep-set eyes, short faces, heavy brow ridges and large, jutting jaws. These so-called ape-like features coupled with their traditional Stone Age culture led Darwinists of the 19th and 20th centuries to imagine that they were some kind of primitive ape-men. The pygmies of Africa fared no better. Many were rounded up and put on display in cages.

Some 19th- and 20th-century Darwinists thought that all non-Caucasian people were ape-like and therefore inferior to whites. Darwin himself wrote that *"at some future period, not very distant as measured by centuries, the civilized races of man will almost certainly exterminate, and replace, the savage races throughout the world. At the same time the anthropomorphous apes...will no doubt be exterminated. The break between man and his nearest allies will then be wider, for it will intervene between man in a more civilized state, as we may hope, even than the Caucasian, and some ape as low as a baboon, instead of as now between the Negro or Australian and the gorilla"* (Charles Darwin, The Descent of Man, 2nd ed., John Murray, London, p.

156, 1887).

Notice how Darwin coupled Negroes and Australian Aborigines with gorillas and contrasted them with Caucasians (despite the fact that Negroes, Aborigines and Caucasians are all 100% human, while gorillas are 100% ape). Essentially, this is what modern Darwinists do with groups like the Neanderthals. Neanderthals appear to have been just another race of humans with superficial *"ape-like"* characteristics like the Australian Aborigines. They appear to have suffered from pathological conditions like rickets and arthritis which exacerbated their superficial ape-like characteristics (rickets is a vitamin D deficiency which softens the bones and can cause people to hunch over). Not only can humans be born with *"ape-like"* traits like heavy brow ridges and large, jutting jaws, but pathologies like cephalic disorders, syphilis, scurvy and rickets can make them look even more ape-like later in life. But everything we know about Neanderthals suggests that they were just as human as modern-day Australian Aborigines. They were skilled hunters, lived in complex societies, buried their dead, and practiced religion.

The bottom line is, deformities and variations within

genomes involve the duplication, misplacement, loss and/or reshuffling of preexisting genetic information and are observed in the natural world and have mechanisms that are identifiable and understood. But the evolution of prosimians into monkeys or monkeys into apes or apes into humans would involve the addition of new genetic information into a genome, a process that has never been observed in nature and whose mechanisms have not been identified by scientists. It's no wonder, then, that we cannot seem to find any real, solid evidence that it ever happened in the past. It is no wonder that the missing link is still missing.

62. QUESTION:
"What is the canopy theory?"

ANSWER: The canopy theory seeks to explain the reference in Genesis 1:6 to *"the waters above the firmament,"* assuming that *"firmament,"* or *"expanse,"* as the Hebrew word is alternatively translated, refers to our atmosphere. According to the canopy theory, there was a canopy of water above the atmosphere until the cataclysm of Noah's day, at which point it disappeared either by collapsing upon the earth or dissipating into space. It is presumed to have consisted of water vapor because a canopy of ice could not have survived the constant bombardment of celestial objects like meteoroids which perpetually barrage the earth's atmosphere.

While Genesis 1:20 (KJV) does say that birds fly in the firmament, suggesting the earth's atmosphere, it also says that the sun, moon and stars reside there (Genesis 1:14-17), suggesting the entire sky from the earth's surface outward, where birds fly and celestial objects reside. The Hebrew word alternatively translated *"firmament"* in some translations and *"expanse"* in others is raqiya. It appears nine times throughout the first chapter of Genesis (in verses 6-8, 14-18 and 20) and eight more times throughout the rest of the Old Testament (in Psalms, Ezekiel and Daniel).

According to Genesis, before there was air or land or any form of life, the earth was a formless mass of primordial water. On the second day of creation, God created the raqiya, placing it in the midst of the water, thereby separating it into two parts: *"the waters above the firmament [raqiya]"* and the waters below it. The waters below the raqiya He named *"sea"* (yam in

Hebrew) and the raqiya itself He named *"heaven," "air"* or *"sky,"* depending on your translation of the Hebrew word shamayim. But Genesis does not provide a name for the waters above the raqiya, nor is there any water above our atmosphere today, assuming that raqiya does mean *"atmosphere."*

Advocates of the canopy theory once speculated that the collapse of such a vapor canopy might have provided the water for the heavy rains which inundated the earth during Noah's flood. It is now known that this could not have been the case, however, due to the latent heat of water and the sheer quantities of water involved. If such a vapor canopy were to collapse into rain, it would literally cook the entire planet. This is because when water converts from vapor to liquid, energy or latent heat is released in the process, causing the surrounding area to heat up; this is known as an exothermic result. Conversely, when water converts from solid form—ice—to liquid or from liquid to vapor, energy is absorbed and the surrounding area is cooled—an endothermic result.

The Genesis account calls for five-and-a-half weeks of constant rain. If a canopy consisting of enough water vapor to provide that amount of rain were to collapse, it would cook the entire planet. This is not to say that there was no vapor canopy or that it did not collapse, only that, if it did, it could not have provided the amount of rain in question (the less water, the less heat).

It is interesting to note that, if a frozen canopy were able to exist in the atmosphere despite cosmic bombardment, its collapse into liquid rain would have an extreme cooling effect and might be an explanation for the commencement of the Ice Age. Despite the fact that we know that it happened, the complex factors involved in getting an Ice Age started makes it seem impossible and baffles modern science to this day. Advocates of the canopy theory also cite the existence of a canopy as a possible cause for a variety of pre-flood anomalies, including human longevity and the apparent lack of rain or rainbows. They claim that such a canopy would filter out much of the cosmic radiation that is harmful to humans and cause the lack of rain or rainbows. However, opponents dispute such a canopy's ability to produce these results.

In defense of the view that raqiya means "atmosphere," the reference in Genesis 1:14-17 to the sun, moon and stars residing there may have simply been a phenomenological statement, just as our modern terms "sunset" and "sunrise" are phenomenological descriptions. That is, we know full well that the sun is stationary and doesn't really *"rise"* or *"set,"* despite our usage of terms implying its movement from our earth-bound vantage point.

Whatever the case may be, there is no canopy up there today and any suggestion that there was one in the past is pure speculation because there simply isn't enough evidence one way or the other, except for the one enigmatic reference to waters above the firmament in Genesis 1:6, and no one claims to know for sure what that means.

63. QUESTION: *"Is the similarity in human/chimp DNA evidence for evolution?"*

ANSWER: In recent years, genome mapping has enabled detailed comparisons between the DNA of humans and that of chimpanzees. Many have claimed that humans and chimpanzees share over 98% of their DNA. This is often taken as decisive evidence of the common ancestry of apes and humans. But is this argument tenable? Is this really a fact which definitively proves a human-chimp common ancestry? It is our contention that the percentage is misleading. In fact, when the data is examined more closely, the human-chimp genome comparisons turn out to contradict what would be predicted by evolution.

In reality, the genetic differences between humans and chimpanzees are probably greater than 2%. More recent studies have shown that the true genetic divergence between humans and apes is probably closer to 5%. Thus, the "over 98% similarity" argument is probably an overstatement.

The differences between the DNA sequence of the human and the chimp are not distributed randomly throughout the genome. Rather, the differences are found in clusters. Actually, at those specific locations, the chimp's genome is similar to that of other primates. It is the human that stands out from the rest. Scientists often refer to these *"clusters"* as human accelerated regions (HAR's) because the human genome supposedly shared a common ancestor with chimps. These HAR's are located in DNA segments that do not code for genes. But this requires us to believe that evolution just so happened to cause such rapid change to occur in sites where those changes make an important difference in an organism's functioning necessary to ultimately create a human.

Such would be a whopper of a just-so story. But it gets better. Some HAR's are found in DNA segments that do code for genes, and herein lies another multitude of difficulties. Evolution would predict that humans evolved from the chimp-human ancestor via natural selection acting on chance variations induced by mutations. However, recent research reveals just the opposite. The HAR's that were found in protein coding genes showed evidence not of mutations that had been selected in view of their advantageous phenotype, but rather the exact opposite. The genetic changes showed evidence that they were, in point of fact, deleterious. They had become established in the population not because they provided some physiological advantage, but in spite of being deleterious. Such results make little sense within an evolutionary framework.

Clearly, the HAR's show a trend in which the differences observed in the human DNA (as compared to similar species) typically increase the G-C content of that particular region of the DNA strand. Evolution would predict that the G-C content of the underlying gene should remain relatively constant, as natural selection picks out the DNA mutations that improve the protein. If evolution is true, therefore, we should not expect a consistent trend toward an increasing G-C content.

These HAR's are not always limited simply to the protein coding part of the gene, but often extend beyond the border into the flanking sequences. This further suggests that these differences which are observed in the human DNA are not, in fact, consequences of natural selection enhancing the protein that the gene encodes. The HAR's often tend to cluster in a single part of a gene, in and around a single exon (as opposed to across the entire gene), and they tend to correlate with male (but not female) recombination. Such observations make little sense in light of evolution.

In conclusion, as interesting as genetic similarities between chimpanzees and humans are, they are not evidence for Darwinism. Design is also able to explain them. Designers often make different products by utilization of similar parts, materials and arrangements. The common percentage pertains to the regions of our DNA that result in proteins. It makes more sense of the data for the Designer of nature to have used the same proteins to perform the same function in a variety of organisms.

64. QUESTION:
"What is the best evidence/argument for intelligent design?"

ANSWER: Modern scientific insight has revealed startling evidence for intelligent design from various disciplines, from biology to astronomy, from physics to cosmology. The purpose of this article is to summarize some of the major arguments.

WHAT IS THE BEST EVIDENCE/ARGUMENT FOR INTELLIGENT DESIGN?—FROM BIOLOGY

In recent years, William Dembski has pioneered a methodology which has become known as the *"explanatory filter,"* a means by which design can be inferred from the phenomena of nature in particular living organisms. The filter consists of a sequence of three yes/no questions that guide the decision process of determining whether a given phenomenon can be attributed to an intelligent causal agency. Based upon this filter, if an event, system or object is the product of intelligence, then it will

1. Be contingent

2. Be complex

3. Display an independently specified pattern

Thus, in order to be confident that a given phenomenon is the product of intelligent design, it cannot be a regularity that necessarily stems from the laws of nature, nor can it be the result of chance. According to Dembski, the explanatory filter highlights the most important quality of intelligently designed systems, namely, specified complexity. In other words, complexity alone is not enough to indicate the work of an intelligent agent; it must also conform to an independently specified pattern.

Among the most compelling evidence for design in the realm of biology is the discovery of the digital information inherent in living cells. As it turns out, biological information comprises a complex, non-repeating sequence which is highly specified relative to the functional or communication requirements that they perform. Such similarity explains, in part, Dawkins' observation that, *"The machine code of the genes is uncannily computer-like."* What are we to make of this similarity between informational software—the undisputed product of conscious intelligence—and the informational sequences found in DNA and other important biomolecules?

WHAT IS THE BEST EVIDENCE/ARGUMENT FOR INTELLIGENT DESIGN?—FROM PHYSICS

In physics, the concept of cosmic fine tuning gives further support to the design inference. The concept of cosmic fine tuning relates to a unique property of our universe whereby the physical constants and laws are observed to be balanced on a *"razor's edge"* for permitting the emergence of complex life. The degree to which the constants of physics must match precise criteria is such that a number of agnostic scientists have concluded that, indeed, there is some sort of transcendent purpose behind the cosmic arena. British astrophysicist Fred Hoyle writes, *"A common sense interpretation of the facts suggests that a super intellect has monkeyed with physics, as well as with chemistry and biology, and that there are no blind forces worth speaking about in nature. The numbers one calculates from the facts seem to me so overwhelming as to put this conclusion almost beyond question."*

One example of fine tuning is the rate at which the universe expands. This value must be delicately balanced to a precision of one part in 1055. If the universe expanded too quickly, matter would expand too quickly for the formation of stars, planets and galaxies. If the universe expanded too slowly, the universe would quickly collapse before the formation of stars.

Besides that, the ratio of the electromagnetic force to gravity must be finely balanced to a degree of one part in 1040. If this value were to be increased slightly, all stars would be at least 40% more massive than our sun. This would mean that stellar burning would be too brief and too uneven to support complex life. If this value were to be decreased slightly, all stars would be at least 20% less massive than the sun. This would render them incapable of producing heavy elements necessary to sustain life.

WHAT IS THE BEST EVIDENCE/ARGUMENT FOR INTELLIGENT DESIGN?—FROM COSMOLOGY

With modern discoveries in the field of cosmology, the concept of a definitive beginning of the cosmos has been demonstrated almost beyond question. The Kalam argument states that

1. Everything which begins to exist has a cause apart from itself.

2. The universe began to exist.

3. Therefore, the universe has a cause apart from itself.

It thus appears from the data that an uncaused first cause

exists outside the four dimensions of space and time, which possesses eternal, personal and intelligent qualities in order to possess the capability of intentionally bringing space, matter— and indeed even time itself—into being.

WHAT IS THE BEST EVIDENCE/ARGUMENT FOR INTELLIGENT DESIGN?—CONCLUSION

This article is but a brief overview of some of the key elements involved in the design inference. The purpose is to demonstrate the wide body of support for intelligent design from a large range of disciplines, including biology, physics and cosmology.

65. QUESTION:
"What does the Bible say about uniformitarianism vs. catastrophism?"

ANSWER: Geologically speaking, uniformitarianism is the idea that geological processes (rates of erosion and uplift, etc.) are essentially the same today as they were in the unobservable past. We can, therefore, make accurate determinations about the past simply by observing the present. This principle is often summed up aphoristically in the phrase *"the present is the key to the past."* A strict uniformitarian would look at a canyon with a river running through the bottom and see millions of years of slow, gradual erosion caused by that river.

Catastrophism is the idea that natural disasters (floods, earthquakes, etc.) can dramatically alter the surface of the Earth very quickly and that we can be certain that at least some of the geological features we see today were formed rapidly during past catastrophes rather than by the slow, gradual processes of uniformitarianism. We must, therefore, take the possible effects of unknown catastrophes into consideration when studying the history of the Earth's surface. A catastrophist would look at the same canyon with the river running through the bottom and wonder if it was the result of gradual uniformitarian or rapid catastrophic erosion (like the canyon rapidly formed by the Toutle River washing out a mudslide following the Mt. St. Helens eruption in Washington State).

The uniformitarianism-versus-catastrophism debate is essentially this: how much can geologists rely on extrapolations of present-day geological processes when postulating the history and age of geological phenomena?

Wile you won't find the words *"uniformitarianism"* or *"catastrophism"* anywhere in the Bible, it is abundantly clear which side it takes in the debate. According to the Bible, the Earth was inundated in a global deluge not many thousands of years ago (Noah's flood). Thus, any geological phenomena caused by gradual uniformitarian processes prior to that catastrophe were either eroded by the flood's waters or else lost under the massive amounts of sedimentation deposited during the flood. We cannot, therefore, rely upon uniformitarian reasoning to take us any further back in time than to the flood of Noah's day. The only canyons we see now are those that were carved out either during the flood or after its waters receded.

66. QUESTION:
"What happened on each of the days of Creation?"

ANSWER: The creation account is found in Genesis 1–2. The language of the Genesis account makes it clear that all of creation was formed from nothing in six literal 24-hour periods with no time periods occurring between the days. This is evident because the context requires a literal 24-hour period. The description specifically describes the event in a manner that a normal, common-sense reading understands as a literal day: *"And there was evening, and there was morning—the first day"* (Genesis 1:5). Further, each sentence in the original language begins with the word *"and."* This is good Hebrew grammar and indicates each sentence is built upon the preceding statement, clearly indicating that the days were concurrent and not separated by any period of time. The Genesis account reveals that the Word of God is authoritative and powerful. Most of God's creative work is done by speaking, another indication of the power and authority of His Word. Let us look at each day of God's creative work:

CREATION DAY 1 (GENESIS 1:1-5)

God created the heavens and the earth. *"The heavens"* refers to everything beyond the earth, outer space. The earth is made but not formed in any specific way, although water is present. God then speaks light into existence. He then separates the light from the dark and names the light *"day"* and the dark *"night."* This creative work occurs from evening until morning—

one day.

CREATION DAY 2 (GENESIS 1:6-8)

God creates the sky. The sky forms a barrier between water upon the surface and the moisture in the air. At this point earth would have an atmosphere. This creative work occurs in one day.

CREATION DAY 3 (GENESIS 1:9-13)

God creates dry land. Continents and islands are above the water. The large bodies of water are named *"seas"* and the ground is named *"land."* God declares that all this is good.

God creates all plant life both large and small. He creates this life to be self-sustaining; plants have the ability to reproduce. The plants were created in great diversity (many *"kinds"*). The earth was green and teeming with plant life. God declares that this work is also good. This creative work takes one day.

CREATION DAY 4 (GENESIS 1:14-19)

God creates all the stars and heavenly bodies. The movement of these will help man track time. Two great heavenly bodies are made in relation to the earth. The first is the sun which is the primary source of light and the moon which reflects the light of the sun. The movement of these bodies will distinguish day from night. This work is also declared to be good by God. This creative work takes one day.

CREATION DAY 5 (GENESIS 1:20-23)

God creates all life that lives in the water. Any life of any kind that lives in the water is made at this point. God also makes all the birds. The language allows that this may be the time God made flying insects as well (or, if not, they were made on day six). All of these creatures are made with the ability to perpetuate their species by reproduction. The creatures made on Day 5 are the first creatures blessed by God. God declares this work good, and it occurs in one day.

CREATION DAY 6 (GENESIS 1:24-31)

God creates all the creatures that live on dry land. This includes every type of creature not included on previous days and man. God declares this work good.

God then takes counsel with Himself, *"God said, 'Let us*

make man in our image, in our likeness'" (Genesis 1:26). This is not an explicit revelation of the trinity but is part of the foundation for such, as God reveals an "us" within the Godhead. God makes man, and man is made in the image of God (men and women both bear this image) and is special above all other creatures. To emphasize this, God places man in authority over the earth and over all the other creatures. God blesses man and commands him to reproduce, fill the earth and subdue it (bring it under the rightful stewardship of man as authorized by God). God announces that man and all other creatures are to eat plants alone. God will not rescind this dietary restriction until Genesis 9:3-4.

God's creative work is complete at the end of the sixth day. The entire universe in all its beauty and perfection was fully formed in six literal, concurrent, 24-hour days. At the completion of His creation, God announces that it is very good.

CREATION DAY 7 (GENESIS 2:1-3)

God rests. This in no way indicates He was weary from His creative efforts, but denotes that the creation is complete. Further, God is establishing a pattern of one day in seven to rest. The keeping of this day will eventually be a distinguishing trait of the God's chosen people (Exodus 20:8-11).

67. QUESTION:
"What is the biblical Creation story?"

ANSWER: The basic creation story is found in Genesis 1 and 2, with the account of the Garden of Eden in chapter 3. Genesis 1 begins before the existence of anything except God Himself. Since this is the case, there is no such thing as a *"pre-historic"* time. God's revelation of Himself and His will for mankind is the beginning. In this beginning, God created everything in the universe in six literal 24-hour days. This includes all the heavenly bodies (including every star and planet), as well as everything on the earth. While the triune nature of God is not explicit in the Genesis account, God does reveal an *"us"* within the Godhead (Genesis 1:26). The Spirit is active in creation (Genesis 1:2) as is Christ (John 1:1-3; Colossians 1:15-17).

In the six days of Creation, God formed the universe and the earth (day 1), the sky and the atmosphere (day 2), dry land and all plant life (day 3), the stars and heavenly bodies including the sun and moon (day 4), birds and water creatures (day 5), and all the animals and man (day 6). Mankind is special above all other creatures because he bears the image of God and has the responsibility to steward and subdue the earth. All of creation was completed in six days in all its vast array and wondrous beauty. The six literal 24-hour days have no time spans separating the days. God announced that His creation was very good. Genesis 2 sees the completion of God's work and gives a detailed account of the creation of man.

The seventh day is marked by God resting. This is not because God was tired, but He rested or ceased from His act of creating. This establishes a pattern of taking one day in seven for rest and sets the number of days in the week still in use today. The keeping of the Sabbath will be a distinguishing mark of God's chosen people (Exodus 20:8-11.)

Genesis next takes a closer look at the creation of man. This passage is not a second creation account, nor is it contradictory to Genesis 1. The account simply takes a step away from a linear report to refocus the reader on God's work concerning man. God formed man from the dust of the earth He had previously created. After forming man, God breathed life into him. The fact that God chose to form man this way shows His great care in this process. God next placed the first man, Adam, in a special place, the Garden of Eden. Eden was beautiful and bountiful. Adam had almost everything he needed including food and productive work. However, God was not done with man.

God helped Adam to see his need for a mate by having him review all the other creatures and naming them. Adam understood that he needed a mate. God caused Adam to sleep and then formed Eve with as much care as he formed Adam. Eve was made from Adam's rib. When Adam saw her, he understood that she was special. She was his counterpart, his complement, and flesh of his flesh. God made both Adam and Eve in his image (Genesis 1:27). This passage establishes the family as the basic building block of society (Genesis 1:24; Matthew 19:5-6.) As a God-ordained institution, marriage is to be only between one man and one woman. Adam and Eve were created in a state of innocence (Genesis 1:25) and had not committed any sin. They enjoyed communion with God in Eden. Part of the relationship was the inclusion of one simple rule. Adam and Eve were forbidden to eat from one tree and only one tree in the entire Garden (Genesis 1:17).

At some point Eve was tempted by the serpent to eat from this one tree, which she did. Adam also ate from the forbidden tree. Adam and Eve sinned against God and lost their innocence (Genesis 2:8-12). Sin brought consequences. God cursed the serpent to crawl forever on the ground and be hated by men. God cursed Eve to pain in childbirth and conflict with her husband, and He cursed Adam with toil and hardship in his labors (Genesis 3:14-19). Part of the consequences for their sin included Adam and Eve being expelled from the Garden (Genesis 3:22-24.) But also included in the consequences is a message of hope. The first mention of the coming Messiah is found in Genesis 3:15. He would come to crush the Serpent (Satan), but not before Satan bruised Him at the Cross. Even in the midst of sin and its dire consequences, God shows Himself to be a God of grace and mercy and love.

68. QUESTION:
"Would the discovery of Noah's Ark be important?"

ANSWER: There have been numerous claimed discoveries of Noah's Ark in recent years. The discoveries have been in various locations, ranging from Mount Ararat in Turkey, to a mountain range in Iran, to an entirely different location on Mount Ararat (with a visitors' center). It is not the purpose of this article to evaluate whether or not the Noah's Ark discovery claims are legitimate. Rather, the question at hand is, if Noah's Ark was discovered, would that be significant? Would the discovery of Noah's Ark cause people to turn to God in faith?

The discovery of a boat-like structure in the mountains of the Middle East, carbon-dated to approximately the time of the biblical account of Noah's Ark (2500 B.C), with evidence of animal life once having been aboard would surely be a tremendous discovery. For those who believe in God and trust in the Bible as His inspired Word, it would be powerful confirmation that the Bible is true and that early human history occurred precisely as the Bible describes it. A verified discovery of Noah's Ark would likely cause many seekers and open-minded skeptics to at least re-evaluate their beliefs. For the close-minded critic and hardened atheist, however, the discovery of Noah's Ark would not make one bit of a difference.

Romans 1:19-20 declares, *"For what can be known about God is plain to them, because God has shown it to them. For His invisible attributes, namely, His eternal power and divine nature, have been clearly perceived, ever since the creation of the world, in the things that have been made. So they are without excuse"* (ESV). If a person is rejecting the clear evidence of God in the universe, no biblically related discovery would change his/her mind. Similarly, in Luke 16:31, Jesus declares, *"If they do not hear Moses and the Prophets, neither will they be convinced if someone should rise from the dead."* No discovery, no argument, and no miracle will change the mind of a person who has been blinded by Satan (2 Corinthians 4:4) and is, with a hard heart and closed mind, rejecting the light of the Gospel.

Conversely, would it matter if Noah's Ark is never discovered? No, it would not matter because the Christian faith is not built on every biblical account being explicitly/conclusively proven. The Christian faith is built on faith. *"Blessed are those who have not seen and yet have believed"* (John 20:29). With that in mind, though, there are two primary explanations for why Noah's Ark might never be discovered. First, the wood of the Ark would have been very valuable post-Flood. Noah and his family would have needed wood to build their homes. It is possible that Noah and his family, or their descendants, deconstructed the Ark and used its wood for other purposes. Second, even if Noah and his family left the Ark intact, approximately 4500 years have passed (if the biblical account is interpreted strictly literally). A wooden structure exposed to harsh elements for 4500 years would, for the most part, decompose/decay into virtual nothingness.

While the discovery of Noah's Ark would be a tremendous and powerful archaeological find, it will never be something Christians should place their faith in. The discovery of Noah's Ark, or the Ark of the Covenant, or the Garden of Eden, or any other biblical artifact will not prove the Christian faith and will not change the mind of anyone whom God is not drawing (John 6:44). *"Faith is the assurance of things hoped for, the conviction of things not seen"* (Hebrews 11:1).

69. QUESTION:
"How do beliefs about creation impact the rest of theology?"

ANSWER: The creation/evolution debate has been raging for years. To many, it seems like two opposing sides yelling at each other with no one really listening. The vitriol has gotten to the point where each side reflexively dismisses the other—evolutionists dismiss creationists as completely ignoring science, and creationists accuse evolutionists of engaging in all sorts of Machiavellian conspiracies to silence their side. This is not to dismiss the arguments of either side as being hyperbolic, but simply to point out that there is precious little honest dialogue going on in this verbal war.

Because of this sentiment, many Christians relegate the creation/evolution debate to the status of a secondary issue, an issue that does not relate to how one becomes right with God through the gospel of Jesus Christ. To a certain extent, this line of thinking is correct. We can get so caught up in this debate that we lose our focus from the main issue—the spread of the gospel. However, as with many other *"secondary"* issues, what one believes regarding creation plays a role in how one views theology in general and the gospel in particular.

Regarding the doctrine of creation, there are several views within Christianity:

1. Literal 24x6 creation—God created all there is in six 24-hour days.

2. Day-Age view—The creation events occurred as depicted in Genesis 1, but instead of six 24-hour days, the "days" of creation represent indeterminate, finite periods of time.

3. The Framework view—The days of Genesis 1 represent a theological framework within which to narrate the creation of all things.

Throughout most of church history, up until the last 150 years, the 24x6 view of creation has been the dominant view of the church. We don't want to believe something simply because it's traditional and historical, including the 24x6 view of creation, but we do want to believe a doctrine because it's supported by the text of Scripture. In this particular case, it is believed by many conservative theologians that the 24x6 view, in addition to having the weight of history, also has the strongest exegetical support from the text. First and foremost, it's the natural view one gets from simply reading the text. Additionally, whenever the Hebrew word for *"day"* (Yom) is accompanied by a numeric modifier (e.g., four days) or the combination *"morning and evening"* (as in Genesis 1), it always refers to a 24-hour day. Finally, the seven-day pattern set forth during creation week is the pattern from which we get our week (Exodus 20:8-11).

Since the advent of modern science, the 24x6 view of creation has been increasingly abandoned by Christians. The primary reason for this rejection is the fact that the 24x6 view of creation necessitates a *"young earth"* age of the universe (anywhere from 6,000 to 30,000 years), and the prevailing scientific view is that the universe is billions of years old. The Day-Age view (sometimes called progressive creationism) is an attempt to reconcile the Genesis creation account with an *"old earth"* view of the age of the universe. Please note that the Day-Age view still posits that God created all things and it still rejects Darwinian evolution, so is not to be confused with *"theistic evolution,"* the view that Darwinian evolution is true but, instead of being guided by blind chance, it was actually guided by the hand of God. However, while Day-Age proponents see themselves as reconciling the biblical account with science, opponents see this view as a slippery slope to rejecting the veracity of God's word.

Because the creation/evolution debate has been relegated to secondary status, there is little or no concern over the theological implications of denying the biblical view of creation (regardless of which view one takes). The conventional wisdom is that it doesn't make a difference whether or not evolution is true. The doctrine of creation is seen as disconnected with the rest of the Christian message. In truth, however, what one believes regarding creation is actually crucial because it goes to the issue of the inerrancy, trustworthiness, and authority of Scripture. If the Bible can't be trusted in the first two chapters, what makes it trustworthy throughout the rest of the book? Typically, critics of the Bible will focus their attacks on the first eleven chapters of Genesis (in particular the creation account). The question is, why? The first eleven chapters of Genesis set the stage for the rest of the biblical story. You can't understand the unfolding narrative of Scripture without Genesis 1–11. There is so much foundational material in these chapters for the rest of the Bible—e.g., creation, the fall, sin, the certainty of judgment, the necessity of a Savior, and the introduction of the gospel. To ignore these foundational doctrines would render the rest of the

Bible as unintelligible and irrelevant.

Yet critics of the Bible and those who have placed science in authority over the Bible want to treat these opening chapters of Genesis as ancient Hebrew myth rather than primeval history. The truth of the matter is that compared to the creation stories of other cultures, the Genesis account reads more like history than myth. In most ancient literature, creation is seen as a struggle between the gods. Most creation myths portray the culture in question as the center of the religious universe. The Genesis account, while sharing many similarities with other creation stories, differs in that it portrays God as the sole Sovereign over creation (not one among many gods) and mankind as the pinnacle of His creation, serving as His stewards over creation. To be sure, there are unanswered questions with the Genesis account, such as the exact date of creation, but the purpose of the Genesis account isn't to give a complete historical account that would pass muster with modern-day historians. The Genesis account was a pre-history of the Jewish people as they were preparing to enter the Promised Land; they needed to know who they were and from where they came.

Another thing to note is that much of Christian theology

is based on the historical accuracy of the Genesis account. The concept of marriage comes right out of the creation account (Genesis 2:24) and is referred to by Jesus in all three synoptic gospels. Our Lord Himself acknowledges that man was created male and female *"from the beginning of creation"* (Matthew 19:4). These references rely on the historical accuracy of the Genesis creation account for them to make any sense. Most importantly, our most cherished doctrine of salvation is dependent on the doctrine of creation and the existence of a literal person named Adam. Twice in the Pauline epistles (Romans 5 and 1 Corinthians 15), Paul links our salvation in Christ with our identification in Adam. In 1 Corinthians 15:21-22, we read, *"For since death came through a man, the resurrection of the dead comes also through a man. For as in Adam all die, so in Christ all will be made alive."* The entire human race is in a fallen state by virtue of being *"in Adam"* through natural birth. In similar manner, those whom God has chosen for salvation are saved by virtue of being *"in Christ"* through spiritual birth. The *"in Adam/in Christ"* distinction is crucial to a proper understanding of Christian soteriology, and this distinction makes no sense if there were no literal Adam from whom all humanity descended.

Paul argues in a similar vein in Romans 5:12-21. But what

makes this passage unique is that it explicitly says, *"Therefore, just as sin entered the world through one man, and death through sin, and in this way death came to all men, because all sinned"* (Romans 5:12). This verse is the linchpin in the argument for total depravity (the *"first plank"* in the Calvinist platform), and like the 1 Corinthians passage, it depends on the existence of a literal Adam for it to make any kind of sense. Without a literal Adam, there is no literal sin and no need for a literal Savior.

Despite what position one takes on the doctrine of creation (24x6 view, Day-Age view, or Framework view), one thing is clear: God created the heavens and the earth. While we believe the 24x6 view possesses the strongest biblical argument, the other two views are valid interpretations within the sphere of Christian orthodoxy. What needs to be stressed is that the Bible does not (either explicitly or implicitly) teach the Darwinian view of evolution. Therefore, to state that the creation/evolution debate is not important is to have a low view of Scripture. If we cannot trust the Bible when it speaks on the matter of creation, why should we trust it to speak on salvation? That is why what we believe regarding creation is important to the rest of our theology.

70. QUESTION:
"Is the concept of Lucifer's Flood biblical?"

ANSWER: There have been attempts by some Christians to reinvent the Genesis account of the creation in order to make it compatible with the theories of modern geology and evolution. Of these attempts, there are three that are most popular: theistic evolution, progressive creation, and the gap theory, from which the term Lucifer's flood, also known as the Luciferian flood, is derived. There is only one reason why Christians attempt to compromise God's Word in this manner—they have accepted the claims of modern geologists and evolutionists that the earth is millions, if not billions, of years old, and they look for ways to squeeze these unfounded millions of years into the Genesis account.

Basically, the gap theory, which for some incorporates the so-called Lucifer's flood, teaches that many millions of years ago God created a perfect heaven and earth (Genesis 1:1). At that time, Satan was ruler of the earth, which was inhabited by a race of men without any souls. Satan rebelled, and sin entered the universe after Satan's rebellion and fall from heaven and

brought God's judgment in the form of a flood named for him—
Lucifer's flood. All the plant, animal and human fossils upon
the earth today were caused by this flood and do not bear any
genetic relationship with the plants, animals and humans living
today. This flood is said to have occurred between Genesis 1:1
and 1:2, and it was this Luciferian flood that reduced the world
to a state described as *"without form and void"* in Genesis 1:2.

The gap theory claims that the earth is very old, possibly
millions of years, based on the observation that rock layers form
very slowly today. The gap theorists claim to believe in a six-
day creation and insist that they are against evolution. However,
the same geologic evidence is used as proof for millions of years
by evolutionists. For that reason, the gap theorists must now
"play" with the Scriptures. They must propose that God literally
reshaped the earth and re-created all life in six literal days, but
not until after a Luciferian flood which produced the fossils we
see today.

But there are some serious problems with this compromise
with the Scriptures. First of all, the gap theory forces millions
of years into the *"gap"* between Genesis 1:1 and Genesis 1:2
without any regard for biblical and scientific accuracy, and then

claims to hold to a literal Genesis. This, in turn, brings up the question of the meaning of the term *"literal." "Literal"* means *"word-for-word accuracy."* Either God's Word is literally true, or it is interpreted. It is impossible to have a literal interpretation; that would be an oxymoron because the two terms are mutually exclusive. If one's interpretation of the Bible is contradicted by another verse in the Bible, that interpretation cannot be correct if we hold to a literal Genesis account of creation.

If God created a perfect heaven and earth, then all life on earth must also be perfect. If this *"perfect life"* was the source of the fossils buried by Lucifer's flood, and sin entered this world by Satan's rebellion, why do these same fossils show abundant evidence for disease and deformities by modern scientific analysis? The presence of disease and deformities in fossils proves that all things could not have been perfect and sin was already present before the flood that buried them. If sin was present before God's judgment of Satan, then either the Bible is wrong or the gap theory is flawed.

If Lucifer's flood was God's judgment against Satan, and the earth was destroyed to such a state that it was without form and void, why did this flood not destroy the fossil record as well?

What about Noah's flood? Gap theorists must assume it had no significance. If Noah's flood was not significant, why is the story of Noah used throughout the Bible to show God's judgment on man, while Lucifer's flood is never mentioned once? How can someone believe that Noah's flood was insignificant and then believe in a literal Genesis?

The truth is that even the Bible shows the problem with the gap theory. Though the Bible doesn't reveal all the details of God's creation in modern scientific terms, to believe modern geologists and evolutionists and their unfounded millions and billions of years is nothing less than believing the words of man (science) instead of the Word of God.

Does it really matter whether we accept a *"literal"* interpretation of the Creation? The answer is *"yes!"* The gap theorists with their concept of the Luciferian flood believe that there was death before Adam, but the Bible declares unequivocally the opposite to be true. Romans 5:12 states that *"sin entered the world through one man, and death through sin,"* so to accept the concept of death before the time of Adam is to destroy the foundational message of the cross: *"For just as through the disobedience of the one man [Adam] the many* were made sinners, so also through the obedience of the one man [Jesus Christ] the many will be made righteous" (Romans 5:19). To advocate the concept of death before Adam sinned is diametrically opposed to Scripture's explanation that death came after Adam sinned and became the necessity for man's redemption.

Genesis records a catastrophe responsible for destroying everything that had the *"breath of life"* in them, except for those preserved in the ark. Christ refers to the global flood in Noah's day in Matthew 24:37-39, and Peter writes that just as there was once a worldwide judgment of mankind by water, so there will be another worldwide judgment, this time by fire (2 Peter 3). The theory of Lucifer's flood is completely without scriptural evidence and must be rejected.

71. QUESTION:
"What was the leviathan?"

ANSWER: There are several references to *"leviathan"* in the Old Testament, but their meaning is sometimes poetic and often obscure. In one instance, the Hebrew word for "leviathan" is used as a synonym for earthly kings and princes, possibly Pharaoh (Isaiah 27:1), and in another instance, it is translated *"mourning"* (Job 3:8). The verses that actually refer to leviathan as a creature don't provide enough information to make a determination one way or the other regarding what type of creature leviathan is. Some commentators believe leviathan is a crocodile because of the references to its scales (Job 41:15) and its use as a food source (Psalm 74:14). Some commentators believe that leviathan is a large sea reptile (not a whale), possibly even a species of dinosaur.

The fact that leviathan is a creature is beyond doubt and, as such, it is under God's sovereign control. God uses the leviathan's strength and power to illustrate to Job his weakness and frailty. God asks Job to consider how powerless he is against even the sea creatures God has created and to understand his position in the universe. God points out to Job that he could never pull the leviathan out of the water with a hook, which would seem to indicate that leviathan could be a whale. Whatever its nature, leviathan is large and powerful enough to be subject only to the sovereign control of the Lord.

Leviathan was a real creature, unlike some of the mythological representations of great sea creatures that do battle with the gods. Leviathan is no myth, but rather a creature of the sea, whether a fish, a sea dragon, a mammal such as a whale, or a reptile such as a crocodile. It is also possible that the leviathan, whatever it was, is now extinct.

72. QUESTION:
"Did God create the universe?"

ANSWER: The scriptural teaching on the origin of the universe is found in Genesis 1:1, which states that in the beginning, God created the heavens and the earth. Steven Hawking attempts to circumvent this truth (or, at the very least, render a Creator logically superfluous to the issue of the beginning of the universe). However, his ideas are not new, but are rather the latest versions of some classic attempts to explain getting something (i.e., the universe) out of nothing.

Hawking's support for his work comes from the existence of the law of gravity. It is known to physicists that the energy associated with the gravitational force is negative, while the energy associated with most ordinary objects (baseballs, cars, etc.) is positive. It is possible for these positive and negative energies to cancel, resulting in zero net energy. Two situations with the same energy (or zero energy difference) are, in a physical sense, equally preferable. An example would be a soccer ball on the kitchen floor; the ball could sit by the refrigerator or the stove or the table without wanting to roll anywhere else. This is because each position on the kitchen floor which the soccer ball could occupy would have the same energy, so none of the positions is energetically preferable to the others.

Hawking envisions the origin of the universe in a similar way. Since it is possible to think of the creation of the universe as a *"zero net energy process,"* Hawking suggests that there is no need to explain how it could have been created. But this inference is based not on the physics, but on Hawking's own philosophical presuppositions. In the example of a soccer ball on the kitchen floor, it is conceivable to imagine the soccer ball sitting anywhere on the floor without needing an explanation; however, it is quite another thing to say that the soccer ball and the kitchen floor came from nothing.

Hawking's attempts to address this problem are not in any way new to philosophers; it is one of the oldest issues in Epicurean philosophy: *"ex nihilo nihil fit" (literally, "nothing comes out of nothing").* Hawking's ideas may establish that two physical situations (the universe existing versus not existing) are energetically equivalent, but it does nothing to address the issue of cause and effect. I don't need an explanation as to why the soccer ball is sitting by the stove rather than by the refrigerator, but I do need an explanation if I see the ball move from the stove to the refrigerator. In physics, a change never occurs without an explanation; in philosophical language, an effect never occurs without a cause.

Hawking's ideas do nothing to address this; the issue of the universe's origin is the same as it was before. It is not possible to get something from nothing. Only the idea of a Creator can adequately explain where the universe could have come from. Moreover, Hawking's statement that science will always prevail over religion *"because it works"* reveals a fundamental misunderstanding of the philosophy of science. Truth is not determined by *"what works,"* but by whether it conforms to the reality around us. When I say that a particular statement is "true," I am saying that the content of that statement actually describes the way things are. This connection between a statement and the reality it describes is independent of me and my mind. A statement may be true or false, irrespective of whether or not it appears to me to describe the correct state of affairs. This is what we mean when we say that truth is objective; a statement's *"truth value"* is a quality which it possesses independently of my knowledge thereof.

However, once we begin to try to decide whether a particular statement is true or false (as happens in both science and religion), the only way we know how to proceed is to try to test the statement to *"see if it works."* As an example, suppose I want to decide whether the statement "All cats are brown" is true. I can begin my investigation by gathering cats together and inspecting each of them to see if any do not conform to the statement in question, thereby rendering it false. I only need to find one gray cat to know that my original statement is false: not all cats are brown.

But what if every cat I was able to find was, in fact, brown? Clearly, the world does contain felines of many other varieties and colors. In this case, even though my statement *"works"* (from my investigation, all cats do appear to be brown), it is clearly false. Thus, the issue of whether science or religion *"works"* is completely irrelevant to the issue of truth in each of these disciplines. While truth can be discovered by noting what works, simply because a statement appears to work does not in fact imply that it is true.

To summarize, Hawking's reasoning fails on philosophical grounds. Hawking attempts to substitute God with a particular physical law (gravity). However, Hawking fails to address the key issue at hand - that is, the origin of physical law in the first place. Where did the law of gravity come from and how does nothing produce something? A physical law is not nothing. Moreover, Hawking's conception of a plethora of ensemble universes to escape the conclusion of fine-tuning is philosophically unsound, metaphysically motivated, and less parsimonious than the theistic interpretation.

Why does man seek to eliminate God from having had any role in the creation of the Universe? It's very simple. Man hates God and does not want to be subject to God's law, or held accountable for his actions. As Paul writes in Romans 1, *"For although they knew God, they neither glorified him as God nor gave thanks to him, but their thinking became futile and their foolish hearts were darkened. Although they claimed to be wise, they became fools and exchanged the glory of the immortal God for images made to look like mortal man and birds and animals and reptiles."*

73. QUESTION:
"Does the Bible teach geocentrism? Does the Bible teach that the Earth is the center of the universe?"

ANSWER: This is a very important question because the answer helps to shape our belief system and worldview, both of which have eternal consequences. The short answer to this question is *"no."* Nowhere in the Bible are we told that the Earth is at the center of the universe. For many centuries, however, people believed that Claudius Ptolemaeus and others were correct when they advocated an Earth-centered universe. They wanted to believe this theory because some thought, incorrectly, that this is what the Bible teaches.

Taken in order, Genesis 1:14-18, Psalm 104:5, Job 26:7 and

Isaiah 40:22 were often cited to support the geocentric theory of Ptolemaeus. Yet none of these Scriptures, taken in any order whatsoever, state that God designed the universe with Earth at its center. In fact, Earth isn't even the center of its own small solar system; the sun is. We can understand why Copernicus and, later, Galileo, who posited the sun-centered (heliocentric) theory, caused such a controversy in the church. It was thought that heliocentricism contradicted the biblical teaching of geocentrism. But, again, the problem was that God's Word doesn't say that the Earth is at the center of anything. Sadly, as time went on and people came to understand that the Earth did in fact revolve around the Sun, many simply lost faith in God's Word, because they had falsely been taught geocentrism.

We must remember that Scripture, not science, is the ultimate test of all truth. How ironic that science has never disproved one word of the Bible, yet it has caused many people to walk away from God. The ever-changing theories of fallible man come and go. Not so with the Word of God, however, as it endures forever (Matthew 5:18). Any time there is an irreconcilable difference between the two, the Bible is where we need to place our faith.

74. Question:
"How does the Cambrian Explosion fit within the framework of young-earth creationism?"

Answer: The earth's crust consists of many layers of fossil-bearing rock. It was once believed that the lowest layer of fossil-bearing rock was the Cambrian and that Precambrian rock was totally devoid of any fossil remains. It is now known that there are actually some, though very few, primitive fossils in the Precambrian. But it is not until the Cambrian layer that we find a sudden burst of life.

The *"Cambrian Explosion"* refers to the sudden appearance of most of the world's known animal phyla, all within a very brief period of geological time (by the conventional standard). The sudden appearance of so many of the major innovations to the basic structures of known animal forms has always been somewhat problematic for Darwin's theory of gradual innovation. But how does the Cambrian Explosion fit with the framework of young-earth creationism?

The old-earth position is that the vast majority of earth's

strata represent long epochs of time, typically millions of years, and that the fossils found in the lower layers evolved before those found in the upper layers. The young-earth position is that nearly all of the strata from the Cambrian period on up were deposited in relatively quick succession as the result of a catastrophic global deluge and subsequent natural disasters, and that the order in which fossils are found is a result of hydrological mechanics (hydrologic sorting for example, the phenomenon whereby dirt spontaneously settles into layers after being kicked up in water).

The conspicuous presence of so many of the world's known animal phyla in the bottom layer does not prove or disprove one position or the other. So young-earth proponents rely on other physical evidences to make their case, including poly-strata fossils (that is, fossils that pass through multiple strata), misplaced and missing fossils and strata, the lack of erosion between strata, the deficiency of bioturbation, undisturbed bedding planes, the limited extent of unconformities, soft-sediment deformation, and well-preserved surface features between layers, etc.

There are, for example, plenty of out-of-place fossils.

Sometimes rock layers containing what are thought to be older fossils are found above rock layers that contain what are thought to be younger fossils (the younger fossils should be on top). The solution for Darwinian geologists is to argue that the strata containing the misplaced fossils were shuffled out of order by some natural geological process. They then reorganize the discrepant fossils and rock layers logically using the assumed order in which the creatures were supposed to have evolved; i.e., this organism was supposed to have evolved before this one, so it goes here on bottom, while this organism was supposed to have evolved after this one so it goes here on top, etc. Darwinian biologists then turn around and use the evolutionary progression organized by the geologists as evidence for the evolutionary progression that the geologists used to organize the strata. This is, of course, circular reasoning.

To summarize, each viewpoint, whether young-earth creationism, old-earth creationism, or Darwinian evolution, struggles somewhat with explaining the Cambrian Explosion. In no sense, though, is the Cambrian Explosion contradictory with young-earth creationism. In fact, young-earth creationism perhaps has the clearest explanation for the Cambrian Explosion, that of the global deluge. Whatever the case, the evidence for the Cambrian Explosion is no reason to doubt the veracity of Genesis' account of creation (Genesis chapters 1-2, 6-8).

75. QUESTION: "What do creationists believe about natural selection?"

ANSWER: Natural selection is considered to be the survival of the fittest and is often confused with evolution. But far from being proof for evolution and against creationism, natural selection is quite a reasonable and *"God-given"* process whereby we observe a certain genotype (the genetic makeup of an organism or group of organisms) that has pre-existed and has gradually adapted to one particular environment. Genes that are pre-existent are those genes that have always been there but certain environmental factors behave as a selection pressure that weeds out other genetic traits that are unsuitable. Hence, those that carry unsuitable genotypes are eventually removed from the gene pool.

The best example of natural selection in a modern-day

environment is the peppered moth, Biston betularia. This moth has adapted through changes in genotype—not the result of random or spontaneous mutation, as evolutionists would prefer—to having two different appearances or *"traits"* within that species. The peppered variety live in the country on surfaces covered in lichen. Their *"peppered"* appearance has developed so as to appear invisible to birds. In the cities, where there is more pollution, the surfaces are darker, and the melanic form dwells there. These two types are of the same species, but environmental factors have predisposed a *"selection"* pressure on each type, so that only one type exists in each particular environment.

Clearly, the peppered moth types were rapidly spotted in the towns, by birds and other predators, and so were easy prey. However, within the pool there were a small number which were dark and less visible and survived to be able to pass on their traits, which in time lead to a *"gene pool"* of predominantly dark moths. The environment only has an indirect effect; the provision of one particular allele leads to the selection of one favorable genotype. This genotype is permitted the survival of the fittest.

It is because natural selection favors *"pre-existent"* genetic traits in any particular environment or situation that enables creationists to agree with the process. Clearly, there are many arguments against evolution, but the very fact that natural selection permits the expression of genetic material that may have never been manifested, due to the effects of being recessive or being diluted due to other, stronger traits, suggests that God has provided the means for survival in changing environments. If anything, natural selection would have been more prevalent after the flood due to the rapid change in climatic conditions. Despite all the consequences that the Fall brought into creation, the Most High had the wonderful ability to foresee the need for a process that would ensure the continuing survival of life on earth, for which He continues to care (Psalm 24:1; Job 12:7-9).

76. QUESTION:
"What is the breath of life?"

ANSWER: The climactic height of God's creative work was His extraordinary creation of man. *"The LORD God formed the man from the dust of the ground and breathed into his nostrils the breath of life, and the man became a living being"* (Genesis 2:7).

The supreme Creator of all the heavens and the earth did two things in creating man. First, He formed him from the very dust of the ground and secondly, He did something to distinguish man from His other creatures—He breathed His own breath into the nostrils of Adam.

We learn three significant facts from this one succinct passage in Genesis. First is that God and God alone created man. Man did not evolve from other creatures. Impersonal forces did not form man. All the cells, DNA, atoms, molecules, hydrogen, protons, neutrons, or electrons did not create man. These are only the substances that make up man's physical body. The Lord God formed man. The Lord God created the substances and then He used them to create man. Man was created and formed by God and by God alone.

The word *"formed"* comes from the Hebrew yatsar which means to mold, shape, form. It pictures a potter who envisions within his mind what he wants to create. This potter has not only the intelligence, but also the power to form his creation. God, then, is the Master Potter who had the image of man within His mind, as well as the power and the intelligence to create man. God had both the omniscience (all knowledge) and the omnipotence (all power) to do exactly what He wanted.

Secondly, God breathed His own breath of life into man. Man is more than dust or physical substance. Man is spirit. We can picture it this way. Man had just been formed by God from the dust of the earth, just a human body lying upon the ground—never having breathed. Then God leaned over and breathed His own breath into the man's nostrils; God breathed into man His own Spirit. This means that God has connected Himself to man in the most intimate way possible. Man is related to God and has the same breath as God, the breath of life.

Thirdly, Genesis 2:7 tells us that man became a living soul (KJV). The word *"soul"* in Hebrew is nephesh meaning an *"animated, breathing, conscious, and living being."* It does not mean the spirit of man. It does mean that he was a living soul just like all the other creatures of earth. However, there was one distinctive difference between the animals and man: man was given the very breath of God Himself, the very Spirit and life of God. Man did not become a living soul until God breathed His Spirit and life into man. As both an animate and spiritual being, man is the only living spirit upon the earth, which makes him unique among all living things.

So what is the breath of God? It is the Spirit of God, given to man to animate him both physically and spiritually. The Hebrew word for spirit is ruach which means wind, breath, air, spirit. Further, the breath of God is the life of God. And the life of God is life that lives on and on, the power to live eternally. God's breath is not temporal; the breath of God lives forever. As such, we, the recipients of the breath of life, will live eternally. The only question is where will we live?

Indeed, God has breathed His Spirit into each one of us. Doesn't it make sense then, that our spirit should breathe after God (Psalm 42:1), that we should long for Him with every breath? For as Jesus, our Lord and our Savior, has promised to all those who believe and call upon His name (Jeremiah 29:11-13): *"Blessed are those who hunger and thirst for righteousness, for they will be filled"* (Matthew 5:6).

77. QUESTION:
"Was Adam and Eve's sin really about eating a piece of forbidden fruit?"

ANSWER: The phrase "forbidden fruit" refers to the story of Adam and Eve in the Garden of Eden. They were forbidden by God to eat the fruit of the tree of the knowledge of good and evil (Genesis 2:9, 3:2). The Bible says nothing about what type of fruit it was. Tradition has identified it as an apple, but it is impossible to know with certainty what kind of fruit it was. From the text of Genesis, every indication is of a literal tree with a literal fruit.

The key element in the passage is not the fruit itself, but the prohibition against eating it. God gave Adam and Eve only one prohibition in His instructions. Whether there was some spiritual property within the fruit is really irrelevant. The sin was in disobeying God's command. By eating the fruit (an act of disobedience), Adam and Eve gained personal knowledge of evil. They already knew good, but now they had the contrasting experience of the evil of disobedience and the guilt and shame that came with it. Satan's lie was that knowing good and evil would make them like gods (Genesis 3:5). In reality, they were already made in the image of God, and had the blessing of His good pleasure.

The lesson for us today is that when God prohibits something, it is for our own good. Disobeying Him, going our own way, or deciding for ourselves what is and is not beneficial to us will always lead to disaster. Our heavenly Father who created us knows what is best for us and when He prohibits something, we should listen to Him. When we choose to obey our own wills instead of His perfect and holy will, things never go well for us. Adam and Eve made that sad discovery after eating the forbidden fruit, and mankind has suffered the consequences of their decision ever since (Romans 5:12).

78. QUESTION:
"What is the meaning of the tree of life?"

ANSWER: The tree of life, referred to in Genesis, is the symbol of God's provision for immortality in the Garden of Eden. Of all the trees that were in the Garden of Eden, two were named for their great importance, but just as one—the tree of life—was a blessing to Adam and Eve, the other was to become a curse for all of their posterity. *"And the Lord God made all kinds of trees grow out of the ground—trees that were pleasing to the eye and good for food. In the middle of the garden were the tree of life and the tree of the knowledge of good and evil"* (Genesis 2:9).

The Lord told Adam that he was free to eat the fruit of any tree in the Garden, except for the tree of the knowledge of good and evil for by doing so he would surely die (Genesis 3:16-17). The tree of life was provided to be continuous reminder that immortality was a consequence of obedience. As long as Adam and Eve were obedient and did not eat of the tree of the knowledge of good and evil, they had access to the tree of life. Once they sinned, they were driven from the Garden, and God placed an angel with a flaming sword to guard the tree of life so they would no longer have access to it. Eternal life was now no longer theirs. Just as God had warned, they died, and through Adam all men after him would die (Romans 5:12).

By barring access to the tree of life, God showed compassion in His omniscience. Knowing that because of sin, life would be filled with sorrow and toil, He graciously limited the number of years men would live. To live eternally in a sinful state with its results—pain, disease, heartache, toil, and grief—would mean endless agony for humanity, with no hope of the relief that comes with death. By limiting our lifespan, God gives us enough time to come to know Him and His provision for eternal life through Christ, but spares us the misery of an endless existence in a sinful condition.

Because God knew that Adam would fail the conditions of his immortality, He provided for One who would redeem fallen mankind. Through one man, Adam, sin entered the world, but through another Man, Jesus Christ, redemption through the forgiveness of sin is available to all (Romans 5:17). Those who avail themselves of the sacrifice of Christ on the cross will see the tree of life again, for it stands in the middle of the Holy City, the New Jerusalem (Revelation 21:2, 22:1-2). Its water is the constant flow of everlasting life from God's throne to God's people.

79. QUESTION:
"How does DNA point to the existence of a Creator?"

ANSWER: Over the millennia, believers in God have marshaled numerous arguments in an attempt to demonstrate God's existence. Various forms of the cosmological, ontological, and moral arguments have been developed and refined with much success. One frequently discussed form of theistic argument has been the argument from design. The design argument has had many notable proponents from Plato to Thomas Aquinas and beyond.

While several versions of the design argument are valid and have been persuasive to many, recent discoveries at the cellular level have provided further ammunition for design proponents. In 1953, researchers Francis Crick and James Watson elucidated the structure of the DNA molecule. In doing so, they discovered that DNA was a carrier of specific genetic information that takes the form of a four character digital code. This information is contained in an arraignment of four chemicals that scientists represent with the letters A, C, T, and G. The sequences of these chemicals provide the instructions necessary to assemble complex protein molecules that, in turn, help form structures diverse as eyes, wings, and legs.

As Dr. Stephen C. Meyer has noted, *"As it turns out, specific regions of the DNA molecule called coding regions have the same property of "sequence specificity" or "specified complexity" that characterizes written codes, linguistic texts, and protein molecules. Just as the letters in the alphabet of a written language may convey a particular message depending on their arrangement, so too do the sequences of nucleotide bases (the A's, T's, G's, and C's) inscribed along the spine of a DNA molecule convey a precise set of instructions for building proteins within the cell."*

The information-bearing properties in the DNA molecule seem obvious. However, does this fact, by itself, force us to infer an Intelligent Designer as the cause of this intelligence? Meyer continues, *"Whether we are looking at a hieroglyphic inscription, a section of text in a book, or computer software, if you have information, and you trace it back to its source, invariably you come to an intelligence. Therefore, when you find information inscribed along the backbone of the DNA molecule in the cell, the most rational inference, based upon our repeated experience, is that an intelligence of some kind played a role in the origin of that information."*

The information-rich features of DNA provide further confirmation that our universe was created and designed by God. As the Apostle Paul said in his letter to the church at Rome, *"For since the creation of the world God's invisible qualities—his eternal power and divine nature—have been clearly seen, being understood from what has been made, so that people are without excuse"* (Romans 1:20). This inspired utterance seems more obvious now than when it was originally written nearly 2,000 years ago.

80. QUESTION:
"What similarities are there between the Gilgamesh flood account and biblical flood account?"

ANSWER: There are many similarities between the Gilgamesh flood account and biblical flood account (Genesis 6–8), beginning most importantly with God choosing a righteous man to build an ark because of an impending great flood. In both accounts, samples from all species of animals were to be on the ark, and birds were used after the rains to determine if flood waters had subsided anywhere to reveal dry land. There are other similarities are there between the Gilgamesh flood account and biblical flood account.

One major point of clear agreement is that a global flooding disaster occurred in ancient times. Portions of the Gilgamesh account (Chaldean Flood Tablets) have been found dating back to 2000 B.C. or earlier. Tablets containing the full story, however, date to approximately 650 B.C., or well after the Genesis account (c. 1450 – 1410 B.C.) These Chaldean tablets, from the city of Ur (modern day Southern Iraq), describe how the Babylonian God Ea decided to end all life except for the ark dwellers with a great flood. Ea, believed by the Babylonians to be the god who created the earth, selected Ut-Napishtim (or Utnapishtim) to construct a six-story square ark.

During the mid-nineteenth century, this complete *"Epic of Gilgamesh"* (from 650 B.C.) was unearthed in some ruins at Nineveh's great library, and the depth and breadth of similarities and differences became evident. Here is a more extensive listing of the similarities and differences:

• God (or several gods in the Gilgamesh account) decided to destroy humankind because of its wickedness and sinfulness (Genesis 6:5-7).

• A righteous man (Genesis 6:9) was directed to build an ark to save a limited and selected group of people and all species of animals (Noah received his orders directly from Jehovah God, Utnapishtim from a dream).

• Both arks were huge, although their shapes differed. Noah's was rectangular; Utnapishtim's was square.

• Both arks had a single door and at least one window.

• A great rain covered the land and mountains with water, although some water emerged from beneath the earth in the biblical account (Genesis 7:11).

• Biblical flooding was 40 days and nights (Genesis 7:12) while the Gilgamesh flood was much shorter (six days and nights).

• Birds were released to find land (a raven and three doves in the biblical account (Genesis 8:6-12); a dove, swallow, and raven in the other).

• After the rains ceased, both arks came to rest on a mountain, Noah's on Ararat (Genesis 8:4); Utnapishtim's on Nisir. These mountains are about 300 miles apart.

• Sacrifices were offered after the flood (Genesis 8:20).

• God was (or gods were) pleased by this (Genesis 8:21), and Noah and Utnapishtim received blessings. Noah's was to populate the earth and have dominion over all animals (Genesis 9:1-3); Utnapishtim's was eternal life.

• God (or the many gods) promised not to destroy humankind again (Genesis 8:21-22).

Perhaps most interesting is how the stories remain consistent over time. Although the complete Epic was discovered in the mid-nineteenth century, much earlier segments (before the writing of Genesis) have been discovered and dated. Yet most significant is the greater fidelity of the Hebrew account. This is attributed to the importance of Jewish oral tradition and the possibility that some of the story was recorded by Noah or from his time, which would make the Hebrew account precede the Babylonian version.

Some scholars hypothesize the Hebrews borrowed the Babylonian account, but no conclusive proof has been offered to support this. Based on the many and varied differences and details within these stories, it seems unlikely that the biblical version depended upon an existing Sumerian source. Further, given the Jews' reputation for passing down information scrupulously from one generation to another and maintaining a consistent reporting of events, Genesis is viewed by many as far more historical than the Epic of Gilgamesh, which is regarded as mythological because of its numerous gods and their interrelationships and intrigues in deciding the fate of humankind.

Certainly, for those who believe the Bible is God's Word, it is sensible to conclude He chose to preserve the true account in the Bible through the oral traditions of His chosen people. By God's providence, Jews kept this account pure and consistent over the centuries until Moses ultimately recorded it in the Book of Genesis. The Epic of Gilgamesh is believed to contain accounts which have been altered and embellished over the years by people not following the God of Abraham, Isaac, and Jacob.

81. QUESTION:
"What is the Day-Age Theory?"

ANSWER: Although Moses wrote the book of Genesis approximately thirty-four hundred years ago, it has been in just the last couple of centuries that serious debate over the nature and date of creation has developed. Consequently, there are now a number of theories relative to the creation account and one of them is called the Day-Age theory. Basically, this is a belief that the "days" spoken of in the first chapter of Genesis are sequential periods and not literal 24-hour days. Each day, therefore is thought to represent a much longer, albeit undefined, period of time, such as a million or more years. Essentially, it is an attempt to harmonize Scripture with theistic evolution.

Science has never disproved one word of the Bible. Nevertheless, in the last century and a half the scientific community has done a remarkable job of indoctrinating us with their worldview, one that is very much opposed to the truth of Scripture. However, the truth is that the Bible is the supreme truth and it should be the standard by which scientific theory should be evaluated, not vice-versa. At the very core of most of these contrived theories is an attempt to remove God from the equation. And one of the unfortunate consequences of questioning the historicity of Genesis is that the floodgates burst open for man to question every part of God's Word that does not agree with our limited intellectual abilities. However, everything Scripture teaches about sin and death requires a literal interpretation of the first three chapters of Genesis. That being said, let's review some of the arguments made by the proponents of the Day-Age theory.

Adherents of this theory often point out that the word used for *"day"* in Hebrew, yom, sometimes refers to a period of time that is more than a literal twenty-four hour day. One scriptural passage in particular often looked upon in support of this theory is 2 Peter 3:8 where it says *"With the Lord a day is like a thousand years, and a thousand years are like a day."* However, as with all biblical interpretation, one must look at the context of the entire passage. In 2 Peter 3:3-10 we see that Peter is talking about scoffers in the last days as they question the second coming of Christ. This passage simply reminds us that God stands outside of time and we should not doubt the occurrence of a future biblical event simply because it seems to be taking a long time from our limited human perspective. Accordingly, 2 Peter 3:8 has nothing to do with the length of the creation week, nor was it meant to turn *"day"* into a mathematical formula.

Each day in the first chapter of Genesis is described as having an evening and a morning. Indeed, these two words—evening and morning—are used extensively in the Old Testament and each time they refer to normal days. Moreover, outside Genesis yom is used with a number hundreds of times—i.e., *"one day"* and each time it means an ordinary day. If Moses wanted to convey a longer period of time he could have used either olam or qedem, in place of yom.

Another reason given for a metaphorical *"day"* as postulated by this theory is that with the sun not being made until day four, how could there have been ordinary days (i.e. day and night) before this? However, the sun is not needed for a day and night. What is needed is light and a rotating Earth. The *"evening and morning"* indicates a rotating Earth, and as far as light is concerned, recall that God's very first command was *"Let there be light"* and there was light (Genesis 1:3). Separating the light from the darkness was the very first thing our Creator did. Also, remember that in Revelation 21:23 we see that the New Jerusalem *"does not need the sun or moon to shine on it"* as the *"glory of God"* will provide the *"light."* At the beginning of creation, God's radiant light would have certainly been sufficient until the luminaries were created three days later.

Additionally, if the *"days"* of Genesis are really long periods of time such as millions or billions of years, then God's Word is completely undermined at its very foundation as we would then have disease, suffering and death before the fall of man, even though Scripture clearly indicates that "sin entered the world through one man (Adam), and death through sin" (Romans 5:12). Thus, it is clear that there was no death prior to Adam's act of disobedience in the Garden of Eden. If this theory were true, it would nullify the doctrine of the fall of mankind into sin. Furthermore, it would also render void the doctrine of the Atonement, for if there was no *"fall"* why would we need a Redeemer?

Martin Luther once said: *"But, if you cannot understand how this could have been done in six days, then grant the Holy Spirit the honor of being more learned than you are...since God is speaking, it is not fitting for you wantonly to turn His Word in the direction you wish it to go."* Instead of looking to science to tell us what God really meant, all we really need to do is study Scripture, daily and eagerly, just like the Bereans (Acts 17:11), as all of it was inspired by God (2 Timothy 3:16), and all of it is true (Psalm 119:160).

Christ Himself spoke of the importance of believing in Moses' writings (John 5:45-47). And in Exodus 20:11, this is what Moses had to say: *"For in six days the Lord made the heavens and the earth, the sea, and all that is in them, and rested the seventh day."*

82. Question:
"How does young earth creationism handle the evidence for millions of years in the fossil record?"

Answer: The *"fossil record"* is a term used by paleontologists to refer to the total number of fossils that have been discovered, as well as to the information derived from them. The problem with interpreting the fossil record is that most paleontologists also subscribe to the theory of evolution. They interpret the fossil record in the terms of a particular theory of evolution, inspect the interpretation, and note that it confirms the theory, which is not a surprise considering the starting point. Creationists, on the other hand, ascribe to the biblical account of creation. How, then, do creationists interpret the fossil record?

To answer this question, we need to begin with the premise that it is impossible for the Bible to contradict true science as God is the author of both. When a fallible human scientist's interpretation of a finding does not correspond with the clear teaching of the biblical texts, we should never reinterpret the Bible, as God's written Word is the final authority in all matters that it addresses. Yet that is what many in the church, as well as others in the Christian community, have been doing for far too long—reinterpreting Scripture to accommodate scientific findings. Consequently, we see a continual erosion of faith in the authority of Scripture.

Clearly, the many contributions made by the scientific community are staggering indeed. In one way or another everyone undeniably has benefited from their research and technological discoveries. However, the fields of paleontology and fossilology are highly prone to error. In the last century we have witnessed countless examples of "ground-breaking" discoveries that have ultimately been proven wrong. Recall, for example, the Coelacanth. Declared extinct for about 70 million years, this fish was thought by scientists to have been the fish that first walked out of the ocean on its way to becoming the ascendant of modern man. One can only imagine the disappointment in the scientific community when a fisherman caught one off the island of Madagascar in 1938. No lungs, no legs. Interestingly, many evolutionists believed the reason this fish disappeared from the fossil record is because they evolved into land-dwelling tetrapods. And here they are, still swimming in and around the Indian Ocean. No lungs, no legs. Yet how many fossils were dated to be roughly 70 million years old simply because their fossilized remains were found in the same strata as the fossilized remains of the *"70 million-year-old"* coelacanth. This is one example why using the geologic timescale to date the age of the Earth does not work.

Next, recall the *"Nebraska Man"* debacle. In the early 1920's a scientist found one single tooth from which he was, amazingly, able to draw an entire picture of what this particular *"ape-man"* looked like. The scientific community was ecstatic. In fact, this tooth was used in the 1925 Scopes trial as proof for human evolution. Two years later, however, other parts of this very same *"Nebraska Man's"* skeleton were found. It was determined that *"Nebraska Man"* was actually an extinct wild pig!

The vast majority of these discoveries come from a worldview that excludes God, the author, creator, and sustainer of life. Any scientific findings, at least those relative to God's creation, made outside the purview of a Christian worldview are suspect from the onset. As the principal methods for dating the fossils and rocks begin with a pre-suppositional paradigm that entails some form of evolution, its findings will often make sense biblically only if we alter Scripture to make them fit. The truth is that our vast fossil record is and always has been compatible with the global flood which God used to send judgment on the Earth. The flood was a violent geologic upheaval with enormous destructive power that not only destroyed all land-dwelling, air-breathing life (Genesis 9:21-23) but also changed the landscape of the entire planet. And the tens of millions of marine fossils found inland on practically every continent certainly dispels the notion of this deluge being *"local,"* as some have argued.

Now, here is what we do know. Fossils represent death. And we further know that sin and then death came about as a result of Adam's disobedience, *"just as sin entered the world through one man, and death through sin"* (Romans 5:12). Now, there is some discussion as to whether or not there was plant and animal death before Adam's sin. However, that debate can be laid to rest when we consider that the last creative work of God was the making of man (Genesis 1:27). And when God finished His work and looked at *"all that He had made"* He deemed it all to be *"very good"* (Genesis 1:31). Now, as numerous fossil discoveries have clearly revealed violence and sickness and disease and even cancer, how possibly could our great and perfect Creator have declared a world filled with such abundant sickness, grief and *"frustration"* (see Romans 8:20) to be *"very good"*?

We further know that Jesus Christ told us Adam was made at the beginning of creation (Mark 10:6), and the genealogical lines given to us in Genesis 5 and 11 reveal the Earth to be roughly 6,000 years old. Accordingly, we can say with God-given confidence that the vast and abundant fossil record we have today was laid down within the last 6,000 years. Indeed, every fossil ever found, then, must have begun the fossilization process after Adam's sin introduced death and decay into our world. Now, of course the secular scientists would certainly deny this, but keep in mind they, for the most part, deny the occurrence of the biblical flood, even though God spent more time talking about it than He did in talking about the creation of the world or the fall of man.

Those who abide in the truth of God's inerrant Word are not the ones who need a paradigm shift. Nonetheless, the world will do its level best to shake us from our beliefs by teaching that truth is only knowable through the changing concepts of science. As Charles Haddon Spurgeon said in 1877: "... *You and I are to take our Bibles and shape and mold our belief according to the ever-shifting teachings of so-called scientific men. What folly is this!*"

OTHER BOOKS AVAILABLE FROM VIP INK PUBLISHING L.L.C.

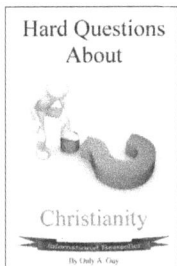

Hard Questions about
Christianity
Only A. Guy
ISBN: 1939670039

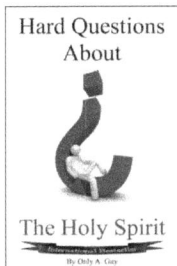

Hard Questions about
The Holy Spirit
Only A. Guy
ISBN: 0984738231

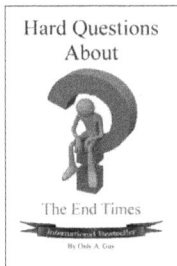

Hard Questions about
The End Times
Only A. Guy
ISBN: 1939670004

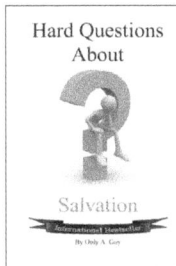

Hard Questions about
Salvation
Only A. Guy
ISBN: 0984738282

For Ransom
Sarah McClain
ISBN: 1939670012

Coming Soon!
Fairytale
Sarah McClain

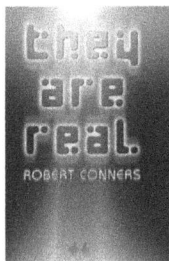

They Are Real
Robert Conners
ISBN: 0984738290

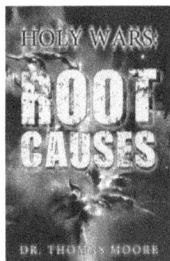

Holy Wars:
Root Causes
Dr. Thomas Moore
ISBN: 1939670020

The Great Deception:
Why Are They Here?
Stanley Simmons
ISBN: 0984738274

www.ingramcontent.com/pod-product-compliance
Lightning Source LLC
Chambersburg PA
CBHW071410090426
42737CB00011B/1416